Rustic *Joyful* Food

Rustic *Joyful* Food

my heart's table

DANIELLE KARTES

Photography by Jeff Hobson & Michael Kartes

Copyright © 2019 by Danielle Kartes
Cover and internal design © 2019 by Sourcebooks
Cover design by Brittany Vibbert/Sourcebooks
Cover and internal images by Jeff Hobson and Michael Kartes

Sourcebooks and the colophon are registered trademarks of Sourcebooks, Inc.

All rights reserved. No part of this book may be reproduced in any form or by any electronic or mechanical means including information storage and retrieval systems—except in the case of brief quotations embodied in critical articles or reviews—without permission in writing from its publisher, Sourcebooks.

This publication is designed to provide accurate and authoritative information in regard to the subject matter covered. It is sold with the understanding that the publisher is not engaged in rendering legal, accounting, or other professional service. If legal advice or other expert assistance is required, the services of a competent professional person should be sought.—*From a Declaration of Principles Jointly Adopted by a Committee of the American Bar Association and a Committee of Publishers and Associations*

Published by Sourcebooks
P.O. Box 4410, Naperville, Illinois 60567-4410
(630) 961-3900
sourcebooks.com

Originally published as *Rustic Joyful Food: My Heart's Table* in 2014 by Lavender Press.

Library of Congress Cataloging-in-Publication Data is on file with the publisher.

Printed and bound in China.
OGP 10 9 8 7 6 5 4 3 2 1

This book is dedicated to

Michael

Thank you for loving me and giving me all that I needed to complete this. Thank you for creating a life together by my side. You are the most tender and patient father, and calm and loving husband. You are my counterpart in the greatest way. The idea that God created a perfect match for me long before we met who possessed everything I lacked and that He brought us together to enjoy life and dream big is amazing in the greatest sense. You amaze me. I love you; you are my heart.

Dianna, My Mom

Be encouraged no matter what you are facing. When my mother was diagnosed with late-stage breast cancer, I was defeated, and it wasn't even happening to me. She shared that God told her to eat what's on her plate. This meant no hiding, no running, and no half-hearted excuses for not doing the recommended treatments.

What a wake-up call. This was it. She was digging in and doing this. She still is; her attitude of gratitude for her life has helped her in beating this disease. Not for one day has she been her diagnosis, and her journey has been hard, to say the least. She has had stays in intensive care, infections, hospitalizations for weeks on end, and death knocking at her door, but she has refused the call.

She taught me how to make stone soup when I was a little girl, and she's taught me how to make stone soup in real life. Dianna Hawkins is the comeback queen, and I have learned that everyone loves a comeback story.

What are you doing this very moment that is keeping you from your comeback? Do you need to face your past, present, or future? I stopped living in my past when my mom got sick, and I am experiencing life now. Her determination to be here for her grandkids is reason enough for me to stop whining and start attacking my dreams not in a way that consumes me but in a way that is just a way of life. I am who God has called me to be: bold and helping others live their boldness as well.

The pie is big enough; there is room for your dreams. Go get them. Thank you, Mom.

Jenny

I have a gift. Her name is Jenny, and she just happens to be my sister. I remember when she first had her babies, long before me, and she was so tender and kind and patient. I always wanted to be a mom like her. She models the kind of mom I want to be for Noah. I have never had a cheerleader like her, or anyone who will laugh as hard over the breeze as Jenny. She is a dose of reality; she is a bunch of dahlias; she is Thai food at 11:00 p.m. for a last-minute second dinner; and she is a cool drink when my heart is parched. She is a gift. She is my best friend. Thank you for everything in this process; you will always be my best.

Contents

Introduction — 1

Pantry Staples — 17

Appetizers — 27

How to Assemble a Cheese Board	29
Bacon-Wrapped Dates	31
Balsamic Reduction, 31	
Black Bean Hummus	32
Sun-Dried Tomato Hummus	34
White Bean Puree	35
Stuffed Roasted Apricots	39
Creamy Artichoke & Spinach Dip	41
Pico de Gallo	43
Spicy Baked Hominy	45
Brie Bruschetta with Seasonal Fruit	47
Rosemary & Bacon Flatbread	48
Tomato Basil Bruschetta	51

Salads & Side Dishes — 53

Asparagus & Cherry Tomato Panzanella — 54
   Balsamic Dressing, 54
Black Pepper Buttermilk Biscuits — 55
Blood Orange, Fennel & Pistachio Salad — 57
Brown Butter Carrots — 59
Heirloom Tomatoes with Goat Cheese — 61
Creamy Parmesan Soft Polenta — 61
Deconstructed Shrimp Niçoise Platter — 63
   Put an Egg on It!, 64
   6-Minute Egg, 64
Frisée Salad with Hazelnuts & Crispy Fried Egg — 67
Herbed Couscous with Avocado & Slivered Almonds — 68
Cilantro Cabbage Slaw — 71
Lentils & Jicama — 73
Orzo with Dill & Tomatoes — 74
Parchment Paper Vegetables — 75
Red Quinoa with Chèvre & Arugula — 77
Roasted Delicata Squash with Garlic — 80
Garlic & Cheddar Corn Bread — 81
Whole-Grain Mustard/Shallot Vinaigrette Potatoes — 83
Rosemary & Tomato White Beans — 84
Roasted Yukon Golds with Asparagus & Rosemary — 87
Strawberry & Goat Cheese Salad — 89
Watermelon Salad with Feta & Cilantro — 89

Soup's On — 91

Beef Barcelona Stew	95
Chicken Sausage Sweet Potato Stew	96
Beef Bourguignon	97
Butternut Squash Soup	98
Creamy Tomato Soup	101
French Onion Soup	102
Pico de Gallo Cioppino	105
Roasted Tomatillo Chile Verde	107
Sister's Turkey Minestrone	109
White Bean, Sausage & Spinach Soup	111

The Main Dish — 113

Angel Hair Pasta with Roasted Summer Veggies	117
Brown Sugar Ribs	119
Caramelized Leek & Bacon Tart	121
Turkey & Chickpea Greek-Style Pitas with Dill Yogurt Sauce	122
Dill Yogurt Sauce, 122	
Cast-Iron Paprika Shrimp	125
Classic Chili with Tomatillos & Grass-Fed Beef	127
Fettucine in Caper & Parmesan Cream Sauce	128
Stuffed Cabbage Rolls	130
Fresh Pasta with White Wine & Butter Sauce	131
White Wine & Butter Sauce, 131	
Ham & Brie Sandwich	132
Spicy Brown Mustard Mayo, 132	
Lemon & Greek Basil Roasted Chicken	135
Farro with Roasted Tomato Vinaigrette & Poached Eggs	137
Roasted Tomato Vinaigrette, 137	
Poached Egg, 137	

Perfect Braised Chuck Roast	138
Spicy Kalamata Puttanesca	141
Wine-Drenched Beef Short Ribs	143
Quick Cashew Chicken	145
Baked Copper River Salmon with Spicy Pineapple Salsa	147
Spicy Sweet Pineapple Salsa, 147	
Thai Rice Salad	148
Strozzapreti in Gorgonzola & Pancetta Cream Sauce	151
Creamy, Spicy Tomato Lasagna	152
Chicken Sausage & Tortellini Pasta Salad	153
Spanish-Style Braised Chicken	155
Hot Dogs	159
Cuban Dog, 159	
Picnic Dog, 159	
Southern Italian Dog, 159	
Kraut Master, 159	
Hot Seattle Dog or Drunk Dog, 159	
The Chicago Dog, 159	

To Drink 161

Blackberry Mint Water	163
Blood Orange Whiskey Cocktail	164
Chilly Hot Chocolate	167
Crème Fraîche Strawberry Bourbon Shake	169
Creamy Bourbon Float	171
Espresso Ice Cream Float	173
Fresh Minted Limeade	174
Cherry Ginger Beer Margarita (Ginger Beerita)	177
Old-Fashioned Drinking Chocolate	179
White Sangria	180
Ginger Lemon Soda	181

Sweets 183

Butter Toffee	186
Almond Pavlova	187
Strawberry Syrup	187
Almond Butter Brownies	189
Banana Bread Made with Greek Yogurt & Pepitas	191
Apple Cranberry Crisp with Vanilla Pouring Cream	192
Vanilla Pouring Cream, 192	
Perfect Apricot & Chocolate Chunk Oatmeal Cookies	193
Bread Pudding	195
Buttermilk Vanilla Pound Cake	197
Brown Sugar Cream, 197	
Chocolate White Chocolate Chip Cookies	199
Infamous Chocolate Sandwich Cookie Buttercream	201
New-School Cinnamon Rolls	202
Coconut Custard Macaroons	205
Cream Cheese Pumpkin Pie Bars	206
Frangipane Jam Tart	209
Citrus Tart	210
Homemade Graham Crackers	211
Creamy Coconut Apple Strawberry Popsicles	213
Dark Chocolate Salted Almond Bark	215
Espresso Crusted Crème Brûlée	216
Cream Scones with Warm Honey & Fresh Strawberry Mash	219
Strawberry Mash, 219	
Lemon Curd, 220	
Strawberry Lemonade Cake	221
Plum Crumble	223
Peanut Butter Ice Box Pie	225
Pistachio Orange Shortbread Cookies	227
Buttermilk Blueberry Muffins with Lemon Shortbread Crumbles & Buttermilk Glaze	229
Buttermilk Glaze, 229	

Blueberry Pie	233
Butter Pie Dough, 233	
Spiced Caramel Apple Pie	234
Strawberry Lime Pie	236
Rhubarb & Raspberry Crisp	237
Bread Pudding French Toast with Strawberry Syrup	239
Stone Fruit Chèvre Tarts	241
Tart Cherry Dark Chocolate Granola Bars	243
Sticky Marshmallow Toffee Cookies with Black Hawaiian Sea Salt	245

Simple and From Scratch   247

Herbed Fresh Ricotta Cheese	248
Lemon Simple Syrup	249
Vanilla Bean Pouring Cream	249
Salted Toffee Sauce	251
Fresh Whipped Cream	251
Plum Preserves	253
Apple Cider Honey Mustard	254
Quick Balsamic & Tomato Jam	255
Quick Sauerkraut	256
Garlic Cheddar Butter	257
Sun-Dried Tomato Pesto	259
Buttermilk Ranch Dressing	260
Sun-Dried Tomato Aioli	261
Herbed Aioli	262
Strawberry Basil Vinaigrette	263
Signature Citrus Vinaigrette	264
Lime Cilantro Dressing	267
Meyer Lemon Caesar Dressing	269

Arugula Pesto	270
Chive Oil	270
Tangy BBQ Sauce	271

Closing Thoughts — 273

Special Thanks — 275

Index — 277

About the Author — 287

Introduction

To feed someone is to love them.

For as long as I can remember, I've wanted to feed people. My young life was in large part shaped by people pouring love and life lessons into my heart while sharing a meal. Every one of my silver-lined opportunities, every heartbreak, joy, and cause for celebration, has been hashed out, mulled over, and laughed and cried about while sharing food with people I cherish. This is the idea that propelled me to write this book.

As I write, I can't help but be overwhelmed by gratitude. I am so very thankful for this life and all God has done for me. I boast not about a perfect life but about an imperfectly perfect life. I am thankful for every one of life's trials, no matter how painful, because together, they've made me who I am today. We all have a special, unique gift to share, and I wish for you to be so bold as to live, doing what you're meant to do.

I grew up modestly in the suburbs of Washington State. There were six of us kids, including two cousins, growing up. I have wonderful memories of long summer nights camping out with neighbor kids in the back of my dad's Ford pickup, berry-picking, or standing waist-high by my mother's side as she mixed cookie dough in a large Pyrex bowl (which she put in the kitchen sink so as to not splatter all about the kitchen).

Scratch-made wasn't trendy when I was a child. It was our normal. I learned a resourceful nature in the kitchen from my mother. She gave me the bones to be an inventive cook.

The way we lived spoke to the tiny chef in me, and I ran with the instruction. When I got older and moved out on my own, I loved calling my mom and asking what went in meatloaf or fried chicken. My mom was my resource long before the internet took over answering my everyday questions.

Flash forward to my midtwenties: I was a newlywed and still adored every bit of cooking, but I hadn't yet found my voice in the kitchen. I was an up-and-coming makeup artist and traveled extensively from Seattle to LA. I decided I needed to be home more, and that's when

I knew nothing about styling food for photography purposes; all I knew was how to make simple, beautiful, seasonal food that tasted amazing with little fuss.

I thought, *Hey, let's open a restaurant!* I obviously didn't know I would be home far less, working in the fast-paced food industry.

I had grown up with a dream of owning a little coffee shop or brunch spot; my sister and I would come up with menus and names all the time. That's where the heart of my restaurant, Minoela, came from: I wanted to own a place that cared for people and nourished their lives as well as their bellies. We had a shoestring budget: my $15,000 and another $5,000 that my husband, Michael, took from his credit card.

We worked tirelessly for four weeks, and then we opened. People said it was unheard of that we got our liquor license in just four weeks and built a meager restaurant kitchen from pieces on Craigslist.

I can remember every detail of the day when we opened the doors to our quaint little organic bistro in the heart of Tacoma's growing theater district. A whoosh of people flooded in, and my tiny kitchen was waiting for orders. A few mishaps and burned crusts later, around midnight, we wrapped day one at Minoela: organic, fresh, scratch-made everything, a New American style of food.

The seasons that would follow, especially the summers, were nothing short of magical. I was sure I had found my calling. We were doing something no one in our area had done: serving farmers' market foods and daily specials of whatever I could dream up in my head, all created and served with copious amounts of love.

Over the next three years, I would learn to be tested, learn what it meant to work hard and run a restaurant, and learn my limits. I grew in ways I never imagined, as a cook and as a person. I learned such a great deal about food while employing some wonderfully talented people. But one thing was missing from my equation: my husband. He continued to work at his job, and we were beginning to grow apart. The daily stresses of owning a beast of a business took a toll on us. I learned that I no longer was who I always thought I was. My heart needed a great deal of work. God knew, too.

At the height of our success, patrons were rolling in, business was booming, and our little bistro had a following of loyal customers, but my marriage was falling apart. And in the middle of it all, I found out I was pregnant. Shortly thereafter, I was placed on bed rest, and my dreams for Minoela came to a close.

Michael took the best care of Minoela and me. He worked at his job sixty hours a week, then served and took care of the bistro at night. With me needing him in a different way, God was softening our hearts toward one another, and I was learning to love Michael the way I always should have. And he was feeling the same way toward me. It's the best thing when you have to let go and let God work out his plan for your life.

In the end, Minoela was too much to keep up with, and four days after our son, Noah, was born, we closed our doors. We held an auction and sold it all, three years of work gone in an afternoon. We cried. But we were together.

I didn't have much time to wallow, because I had this precious new life to tend to, this bright spot in a dark time. Over the following year, Michael and I would learn how to be parents and how to love each other the way God intended. In the midst of losing all our earthly comforts, including our house, we managed to fall more deeply in love and stay with each other. We came back together by the grace of God and began to have fun again, now as a family. Noah brought out parts of us we never knew existed. I am so grateful He trusted us with this tiny miracle.

After Minoela closed, I didn't cook. I prepared food, but I didn't create. I closed up that side of myself and put my head down as we cleaned up the failed-business mess. I decided the part of my life that adored cooking must come to an end.

I sure do love it when we make plans and God has another. When my precious boy was three months old, I went back to work, doing weddings and makeup and traveling. I didn't tell anyone we had owned a bistro. I wanted to pretend it didn't happen and that those three years were a mistake.

Spring came the next year, and with the proverbial thaw came a thaw in my heart. There was a creative side I learned to quiet while I was learning how to live again as a wife and mother. I loved cooking. I loved people. I loved my baby. And as he started to eat real foods for the first time, I found myself dreaming up

> *We may have lost our earthly possessions, but we gained family and love. I realized what matters and stopped striving solely for success.*

tasty, nutritious things for Noah: roasted apples and plums whirred together with sweet potato or zucchini. He was such a sweet baby and happily tried my creations. I was so excited to feed him.

This new desire to cook permeated my home. I started dreaming again. I brought treats to work. People said, *Wow! You should own a place!* How little they knew. I started to tell a few coworkers about my business, but not many. My husband missed the food we had made at Minoela, so I started cooking it again. It was a happy time; we had very little, but we were in love with each other and with our sweet boy. We really were moving on.

Still, there was a small idea in my mind I kept trying to push away, an idea I tossed around many times during the heyday of Minoela: a cookbook. I would scribble down titles and ingredients on guest checks, and my mom would write out some of my specials so as not to forget them. She was so great: *Danielle! Tell me EXACTLY what's in this so we can remake it!* I'd call out the list, and a recipe for something magical was born.

I managed to keep most of those scribbles. I knew in my heart it was time to start, but I knew nothing about writing a book!

I went to high school with one heck of a guy, Jeff Hobson. Jeff had become a local celebrity of sorts in the photography world, and I knew that if I was going to embark on this project in earnest, he might just be the guy to help me set sail. I knew nothing about styling food for photography; all I knew was how to make simple, delicious food with little fuss. So I called Jeff.

We sat in a crowded Starbucks, my favorite cookbooks in tow, and he held Noah while I pitched my idea. We had no money, but I had heart. I've always had heart. Over the next two years, Jeff taught me how to style food, a lot of which had to do with just being myself and preparing dishes like we'd serve them. We planned shoot after shoot, upwards of ten dishes in three to four hours' time. They were a whirlwind, but I came up with many Minoela recipes and all my homemade favorites as well. God was using this project to heal my heart.

We wrapped the book in the summer of 2013, and I was sure it was ready. Two rejections later, I thought maybe I'd just let it rest a bit.

> *There was a creative side I had learned to quiet during the time while I was learning how to live again as a wife and mother first.*

I'm not a traditional stylist. I don't use gimmicks or tape or glue—it's all just beautiful food, shot then devoured on-set or in my living room.

My mom was diagnosed with late-stage breast cancer at the same time. Everything we had dealt with in loss pales in comparison when someone you love so much falls ill. She has boldly endured grueling treatment, and I am happy to say she is thriving. Her journey is an example of determination.

I have never been closer to my sister and mother than I am now. Sickness can bring out the ugly, but we don't think of the beauty it renders in our hearts. It's shown us how to love and, more importantly, how to live.

Jeff, now one of our best friends, had also fallen ill, with leukemia, but you can never understand the word *fight* until you've walked along with Jeff and his family. He is facing daily treatments head-on, and God is healing him.

This last year was scary, but we serve a mighty God. Another silent year for the book came and went, but I didn't mind. Our family had banded together in support of healing. We never stopped living; we lived even more fiercely!

I am learning how each day is a gift. Every day is an opportunity to love without regret. If you had asked me five years ago what Michael and I had planned for our lives, I might have rattled off dreams and ideas of grandeur that had little or no meaning. Today if you asked me where I hope to be in five years, I am confident I would say: happy.

I don't think I ever thought of myself pursuing a career in food styling, recipe writing, or food photography, but it sure is a blast. It happened so gradually over the past few years rebuilding, relearning, and just allowing life to happen, really.

Food-styling opportunities presented themselves, and before I knew it, I got a feature on the cover of a local magazine! I began writing and developing for several publications, and at the same time, Michael took his years of interest in and love for photography and went for it, launching a business as a professional photographer.

The book hadn't done much except run across my mind here and there when coworkers would ask. I knew I was where I was supposed to be. This entire process for me was very organic: I never set out to make beautiful pictures, but I was able to fully step into my purpose in life once I let go of all I thought I was *supposed* to become.

Being a stylist is wonderful, frustrating, creative, and passionate all at once. Michael and I are able to do projects together. Often, I'll make dinner, set up the shot, and, a few clicks later, we're eating that prop for our meal! It's hilarious and such a blessing.

I'm not a traditional stylist. I don't use gimmicks or tape or glue; it's all just beautiful food, shot then devoured on-set or in my living room. These years have taught me how to grow, how to love, how to be graceful, how to be kind, and how to be humble. When you lose your earthly possessions but gain family, love, and perspective, you realize what matters, and you stop striving solely for success. At this point in our lives, when successes come, I am thrilled, but they don't define me or who I am. Success is great, but it doesn't give the kind of joy I get from loving people, or the kind of joy I get from holding my son's hand or dating my husband. We've learned how to enjoy each other, how to love each other with everything we have, and how to love the Lord together.

You see, life is filled with trials, and if we can harness who we are in the Lord, we really are unstoppable. Bad things might happen, and we might feel like it's too painful to endure, but in that pain, new life is being wrought. In the discomfort of failure, new life is beginning. Don't let anything stop you from your dreams: not loss, not failure, not sickness.

I invite you to make these recipes until the binding of the book breaks. Know they are truly heirlooms: rustic, joyful food. Please pull up and eat at my heart's table.

In the discomfort of failure, new life is beginning. Don't let anything stop you from your dreams.

March 2019

It's been six full years since I wrote the original introduction to *My Heart's Table*. Six whole years of healing and life have taken place. At the time, I had no idea why it felt so imperative in my heart to get this book out, but now I know: writing this book opened a door to healing my heart in a way I never could have imagined. Writing this book gave way to a career I am so grateful for, in writing, food styling, and speaking.

Being able to share about my family's struggles following the loss of our home, our cars, and our livelihood has led me to hugging and praying with complete strangers after they hear my story. None of that would've happened had I not been vulnerable and open with my pain, even in the midst of it. I can remember speaking at churches and asking the ladies in the room or on the church stage what they had planned for. What dreams were broken? If their marriages were hurting. I'd hold my book up and let everyone know that creating this book was a product of living through brokenness and hurt. That it was a culmination of broken dreams. That my broken years were planting seeds of hope in my heart that would become unshakable oaks in my life. The years we spent struggling grew and refined me, taught me that God had a plan and a purpose and that he was surely with us, always.

I had no idea what those photo shoots in my living room and the production of this book would give way to. We crowd funded the project by preselling copies of a book that wasn't even printed yet, just to get it off the ground. It took selling a mere two hundred copies via social media to pay the designer, the publishing fees, and the editor. When I held it in my hands for the first time, I was

INTRODUCTION 9

Following the closure of our restaurant, Minoela, in 2011, our life became so much simpler.

in awe of what had come out of our hearts and little apartment. And the book, finally realized, wasn't even the high point.

During this time, I learned that my husband, Mike, is one of the most incredible men I've ever had the privilege of knowing. Not because he's perfect or because we are #blessed or because he's the best or better than anyone else's husband, but because he is perfect for me. We are the truest friends. We share a life, wonderful and messy at times, melded together by joy and pain and children and memories. So many of our early marital struggles were driven by selfishness and an inability to see the forest for the trees. Once we stopped chasing and attempting to recapture the childish sparks from our dating years, it allowed God to build a fire between us that made our relationship deep and full and sacred. I'll take a fire over a spark any day of the week and twice on Sunday! The process of building our boutique photography, food styling, and writing business, Rustic Joyful Food, has given us something to look forward to each day, something we can build together, using both of our skill sets in an unselfish way.

Following the closure of our restaurant, Minoela, in 2011, our life became so much simpler. Raising Noah was a breeze and a joy compared to all we'd been through with the business. He continues to be a joy, bringing out so much in us as parents that needs refining and healing and extra self-attention. He makes us laugh at ourselves and the world around us. He reminds us why we love each other. Parenting has been the ultimate reminder of just how much God cares for us and loves us.

In January 2017, Mike and I found out we were expecting another baby! How'd this happen? Well, I knew how it happened—ha!—but honestly, it was the furthest thing from my mind. My career was ramping up. We had food styling and photography workshops planned in France and New York City. So much work to be done! Well, I figured, guess I'll just have to do the work pregnant. When we told Noah he was going to be a big brother, he squealed in delight and said, "Mama, I prayed for this baby! Oh, Mama, I prayed for a baby!" I had prayed for another baby, too, but was taken by surprise nonetheless. It's funny how God hears our hearts and never forgets, even if we set the prayers down.

My pregnancy with Milo became very difficult early on. When I met with my doctor, he was very matter-of-fact: "We will just have to put you on a shelf. You are a porcelain doll for the next seven months. No lifting, no bending, certainly no working. No travel." So, on a shelf I went.

I almost completely stopped working. Fewer and fewer food shoots, less traveling and speaking. It felt a lot like when I was on bed rest and Minoela started to fail. My bed rest meant fewer opportunities. Mike continued to work his day job, and we were doing fine financially, but I was so sad and was hoping so hard for our sweet boy to arrive safely.

Milo was born via emergency surgery on July 15, 2017, eight weeks early. During a long recovery for both of us, I had the feeling it was time to finish my second book, *Generations*. In the two years since launching my first book, I had begun to casually write the follow-up. I wanted to further share my point of view, stories from my childhood, and more about where I came from. I said out loud in my dark hospital room, "Now, Lord?"

With what capacity? With what money? I have had this feeling a few times in my life. The urgency was a calling I couldn't ignore. We brought Milo home four weeks after he was born, and I began writing. I wrote and wrote. Tears streamed down my face as I healed through the process of writing *Generations*. The sadness I felt was palpable. I knew if I kept pushing, I'd come out of it. I was mourning the way I thought my year should have gone. I was mourning the way Milo had been born. My hormones wreaked havoc on my mind, and slowly but surely, the further away I lived from the experience, the less often it took my breath away. It didn't make my heart race as much.

God has this perfect plan. My creative outlet became my medicine. I'd give Milo his night feeding around 9:00 p.m. and hold him while he slept for three hours, until his next feed. During that time, I wrote. On my phone and on my laptop. *Generations* was self-published and released to the world in November 2017.

People were shocked. *How'd you write a book? How'd you do this with everything you had going on?* The fact is, we just worked hard and tirelessly. Nothing ever came easy, but that

didn't mean it wasn't the work we were called to. The greatest lesson of my life's most difficult experiences, I am convinced, is that people, everybody, *can do this*, whatever it is. We were made for hard things.

This season, moving forward has given me a perspective I didn't know I required. I needed these years like water or air. I needed to so fully lean into the Holy Spirit that there would be no separation from my need for the Lord in my life. Man, this kind of letting go I can only compare to the rain. Rain cleanses. Tears heal. There is treasure in the desolate winter, treasure that can only be produced after a freeze, after what seems hopeless and barren and lifeless. Then, all of a sudden, as if in an instant, a bloom sprouts from the ground. It takes its time, but it's always right on time. Even when you're certain it isn't, your treasure is coming. We've stepped out more in faith than I ever have, now with a new baby. We continue to grow our company and take on new tasks and challenges. Mike now works with me full-time; together, we are Rustic Joyful Food.

Self-publishing can be a roller-coaster ride of emotion, but one moment stands out in my mind and defines this whole journey for me. While promoting *Generations* in New York City, Mike and I needed a good cup of coffee to get our minds right before an appearance on a national television show. We stopped into a shop about a block from our hotel. Just ahead of us in line was a man who appeared to be homeless. He ordered a hot sandwich and a drip coffee. The woman behind the counter told him his total, somewhere around seven dollars. He held out a hand containing a dollar bill and some change. He humbly said, "Ma'am, all I have is $1.37 and I am hungry."

The woman behind the counter didn't miss a beat, boldly singing out, "I got you!" He stood there, stunned. She repeated herself, whispering this time: "I got you." Her coworker quickly picked up on what was happening, and with his Brooklyn accent said, "Nah nah, man, don't worry about it. We got you today! Keep it movin', brother. I'll meet you at the end of the bar with your goods." The man shuffled forward, and we were next.

I stepped out of line to hide my tears. All I could feel was the

In the two years since launching my first book, I had begun to casually write the follow-up. I wanted to further share my point of view, stories from my childhood, and more about where I came from.

gentle pressing of the Holy Spirit letting me know: I got you. Some days you need to just bring what you have, even if it's not enough. Jesus has you. He's got you in the palms of his hands. You may very well be in the fight of your life, taking back your ground, rediscovering who He made you, who He called you to be. Joy is not without sorrow, but its presence is a gift in the midst of it all.

I am continuing to stretch and laugh and share. In the fall of 2018, we were presented with the opportunity to do something I had longed to do, and together with our new publisher, we have released this second edition of *My Heart's Table*, a true and settled look at what restaurant life, early marriage, and motherhood are like. You are truly catching a glimpse into my world as a cook, a mother, and a hopeful mess. It's a collection of recipes and stories, an honest look at food and life as I've lived it over the last ten years. In addition to the re-release of this volume, we will also be re-releasing *Rustic Joyful Food: Generations* and, in time, a third book in the Rustic Joyful Food series. So here we are, reliving, reshooting, and breathing new life into the book you hold in your hands. These last five healing years are just a foreshadowing of what is still certainly to come: a lot of grace and hard work and memories. We will always laugh, we will always work hard, and we won't ever take for granted the fact that life is good *right now*, not when you have the best of everything, possess that pretty kitchen, or work at that perfect job. Life is, and has always been, messy and truly good.

Pantry Staples

I'm hoping to simplify and demystify things in your cooking world.

Cooking may feel overwhelming for some: the list of ingredients, the recipes that need to be perfect, the timing, etc., etc....
    I'm hoping to simplify and demystify things in your cooking world. I'm not a chef, nor have I ever been formally trained. I've learned many beautiful things over the years through self-study and working alongside the chefs I was lucky enough to employ. And I've learned that if you stock your pantry regularly with certain key items, recipes will never seem too far off from fully coming to life in your own kitchen.
    I'm one of those folks who like variety and fresh local foods. My style of cooking just happens to favor New American cuisine: a melding of typically French and Italian influence but with a new-school twist, lots of fresh ingredients, and an American flare.

In My Pantry

In my pantry, I always have a few oils to get the job done:

Olive	Grapeseed
Canola	Coconut

Olive oil is wonderful when you want flavorful oil for pestos or when you're using lower cooking temperatures. It's also heart-healthy.

Canola oil I use strictly in baking or frying, and recently, I've been using coconut oil in recipes where I need a higher temperature for a sauté, or even in baking.

I use oils that are good for your heart. I tend to stay away from vegetable oil, margarine, or shortening.

I usually season with olive oil, sea salt, and black pepper. But about 50 percent of the time, I look to my seasonings for a boost of flavor.

I prefer fresh herbs but always have a nice mix of dried herbs on hand:

Garlic powder	Black and pink	Paprika
Onion powder	peppercorns	Chili powder
Dried basil	Onion powder	Cumin
Sea salt	Turmeric	
Black lava salt	Cinnamon	

PANTRY STAPLES

Remember, these are only building blocks. I pick up new items all the time, but if you try to always have the basics on hand, it'll be very easy to achieve any recipe. Here are a few of my favorite basics:

- Diced, stewed, and whole tomatoes
- Several varieties of beans, dry and canned
- Curry pastes
- Unsalted beef and chicken stocks
- Brown and jasmine rice
- Dried whole-grain pastas
- Quinoa
- Vinegars: white, champagne, balsamic, rice, and apple cider
- A few types of nuts
- Almond, hazelnut, and peanut butters
- Baking soda, flours, and baking powders
- Chocolate chips
- Honey
- Jams
- Marinara sauce

My refrigerator always has a few items, too, and I largely leave the fresh part open for the imagination! But here are a few items you'll find without fail:

- Garlic
- Onions
- Carrots
- Spinach
- Lettuces
- Celery
- Potatoes
- Fresh herbs (cilantro, flat-leaf parsley, and rosemary)
- Citrus (lemons, oranges, and limes, without fail!)
- Dairy products (buttermilk, whole milk, and sour cream)
- Butter (this needs recognition all its own!)
- Eggs
- General condiments: mustards, capers, and sauces
- White wine (this might be the single most popular item I use for cooking!)
- Fresh meats (I don't like to freeze meats too often unless I have to, so I shop weekly and buy only what I need, such as chicken, ground turkey, fish, and beef)
- Cheeses (I like to have a variety, such as blue, cheddar, and parmesan, but the cheeses are always rotating!)

My pantry is far from perfect, but it holds the building blocks for great meals! When you're in the mood to create my tasty flatbread, for example, you'll need to purchase only three or so of the seven ingredients called for, because you're always drawing from and replacing your pantry staples!

Appetizers

There's nothing better than serving something inspired and simple to the people I care for.

Every day, someone I loved would stop into Minoela, and that would be my cue! There's nothing better than serving something inspired and simple to the people I care for. It could be anything: roasted potatoes, fresh small salads, or farmers' market vegetables. There's no better feeling than setting food before people who don't even know they need it and hearing them gush with excitement over how delicious it tastes! Every appetizer in this section was served at Minoela.

Sometimes, I got to know people's stories through these dishes. For instance, the tomato bruschetta! There was one sweet couple in particular who came in after being married at the courthouse down the street. The woman wore a sweet, simple lace dress and he was in a suit. He was in the military, set to be deployed in the coming weeks, and they chose to enjoy their first dinner as husband and wife at my bistro.

I brought them everything, even things they didn't order. And when they began to eat the bruschetta, they were overjoyed! When it was time to deliver the bill, I sent a little note that said *Here's to your happily ever after! Dinner is on the house.* The bride said that nothing she'd ever eaten tasted so good. They left, thrilled, and headed down the street and into forever. Watching them go, my heart was full.

Time passed, and that new bride would stop into Minoela every so often for a plate of bruschetta, and I'd pour her a glass of viognier. She told me once that each time she ate this food, she felt she was with her new husband and that he wasn't very far away. To feed someone's life like that gave me all the hope I ever needed.

How to Assemble a Cheese Board

I love to entertain, and I love cheese. My girlfriends and I love a good gossip session and large hunks of cheese to go with it. OK, maybe not gossip, but just a good time to catch up.

OPTIONAL INGREDIENTS

Parmigiano Reggiano
Brie
Camembert
Roquefort
Gorgonzola
Chèvre
Triple-cream Brie
Honey
Jams, chutneys, or cutting preserves
Any fresh, crisp fruits (apples, pears, etc.)
Apricots
Dates
Cashews
Pecans
Olives
Chocolate
Crackers
Tomatoes
Charcuterie meats (prosciutto, salami, mortadella, etc.)
Smoked or cured sausages
Medium-rare thinly sliced steak
There are no right ingredients; be creative!

DIRECTIONS

I think every great board needs at least 3 styles of cheese, plus a sweet, savory, and salty element to feel complete.

I like to include a hard cheese such as Parmigiano Reggiano, a medium or semisoft cheese like Brie or Camembert, a pungent cheese like Roquefort or Gorgonzola, and a soft cheese like chèvre or triple-cream Brie.

For the sweet part, dollop a few tablespoons of honey right on the board (fig jam is also the TRUTH). Add crisp fresh fruit, like tart Pink Lady apples or red pears, then maybe a dried fruit like Turkish or Californian apricots or dates.

Now you need a salty element, such as toasted nuts. Cashews or pecan halves are lovely. And you can't go wrong with olives. Uncured olives are soft in flavor and pair great with everything we've chosen.

Be creative! The name of the game is to definitely inject your personality onto your cheese boards every time! Brush up on where your cheeses come from to add a layer of conversation to your relaxing evening.

APPETIZERS

Bacon-Wrapped Dates

PREP TIME: 10 minutes COOK TIME: 15 minutes SERVES: 4

Bacon-Wrapped Dates

You're going to be a superhero at every party you take these to. In fact, some people might even ask to see your cape! I love these as the star of a simple mesclun salad dressed with Signature Citrus Vinaigrette (see recipe page 264) and Balsamic Reduction.

INGREDIENTS

10 slices thick center-cut bacon
20 pitted, dried dates
20 1-inch cubes or chunks Irish cheddar cheese
20 pecan halves
½ cup Balsamic Reduction (see recipe below)
20 toothpicks

DIRECTIONS

Preheat the oven to 425° (use convection setting, if available). Slice the bacon in half, and set aside. Stuff each date with 1 piece of cheese and 1 pecan half. Wrap each stuffed date with half a slice of bacon, making sure to cover the cheese end of the hole. Use a toothpick to secure the bacon. Place a wire cookie rack on top of a cookie sheet. (This allows the fat to drip away from the snack and provides a crispier treat.) Bake for 15 minutes, flipping once. After removing from the oven, drizzle with Balsamic Reduction and serve immediately.

Balsamic Reduction

2 cups balsamic vinegar (yields 1 cup)

DIRECTIONS

This is such a great recipe. Only one ingredient! Place the vinegar in a medium saucepan. Open your windows and try not to breathe in the pungent fumes while it reduces. Simmer over medium to medium-high heat for about 15 minutes, until reduced by half. Cool completely on the counter and store in the fridge for up to eight weeks in an airtight container. Bring to room temperature before use. This is a wonderful addition to every salad that needs a sweet, tangy bite!

PREP TIME: 5 minutes **SERVES:** 4

Black Bean Hummus

INGREDIENTS

1 (15-ounce) can black beans, drained but not rinsed
¼ to ½ cup olive oil
2 tablespoons tahini
Juice of 1 lemon
1 large clove fresh garlic
1 teaspoon freshly cracked black pepper
1 teaspoon garlic powder
1 teaspoon lemon zest
1 teaspoon Sambal chili paste
½ teaspoon red pepper flakes
½ teaspoon sea salt
½ cup crumbled feta

DIRECTIONS

In the bowl of a food processor, combine all the ingredients. Pulse until a smooth and creamy dip comes together. Taste for spice, adding where necessary. Serve with fresh veggies and toasted pita chips. Top with crumbled feta.

PREP TIME: 5 minutes **SERVES:** 4

Sun-Dried Tomato Hummus

INGREDIENTS

2 (15-ounce) cans garbanzo beans or chickpeas, drained
¾ cup sun-dried tomatoes packed in olive oil
Juice and zest of 1 lemon
1 clove fresh garlic, smashed
2 tablespoons cold water
1 teaspoon freshly ground black pepper
1 teaspoon onion powder
1 teaspoon Thai chili paste
1 teaspoon sea salt
½ teaspoon red pepper flakes
1 cup olive oil

DIRECTIONS

In the bowl of a food processor, combine garbanzo beans or chickpeas and all the ingredients except the oil. Pulse until combined; slowly add oil through the pour spout on top of the lid. (The slow incorporation of the oil makes for a creamy dip.) Continue to mix in the food processor at least 3 to 5 minutes or until desired consistency. The more you blend, the creamier this dip will become. Hummus should be bright and full of flavor! Serve with soft pita or fresh veggies.

PREP TIME: 5 minutes **SERVES:** 4

White Bean Puree

[This is wonderful as a dip or as a base for fish or chicken!

INGREDIENTS

1 (15-ounce) can cannellini beans, drained and rinsed

2 tablespoons olive oil

Squeeze of fresh lemon juice

1 clove fresh garlic

1 teaspoon freshly ground black pepper

¼ teaspoon red chili flakes

¼ teaspoon salt

DIRECTIONS

Simply add all the ingredients to the bowl of a food processor, and mix until creamy and smooth. Add more lemon juice or oil for your desired flavor and consistency.

PREP TIME: 10 minutes **COOK TIME:** 15 to 20 minutes **SERVES:** 4

Stuffed Roasted Apricots

> When these little, beautiful gem apricots were in season, we would make hundreds of them at Minoela. You just stuff, wrap, and roast them until they are jamlike in consistency. This show-stopping appetizer can double as a meal with a crisp glass of white wine.

INGREDIENTS

6 small, ripe, firm apricots
½ cup brown sugar
½ cup chèvre (goat cheese)
12 slices thick center-cut bacon
Honey to finish
Balsamic Reduction (optional; see recipe page 31)

DIRECTIONS

Preheat the oven to 425°. Slice the apricots in half, and discard the pits. Stuff each half with 1 teaspoon brown sugar, and cover the sugar with 1 teaspoon chèvre. Wrap each apricot in 1 slice of bacon, and roast on a lined baking sheet for 15 to 20 minutes or until the bacon is crisp and browned and the apricots are cooked through. Drizzle with honey and/or Balsamic Reduction if desired.

PREP TIME: 5 minutes **COOK TIME:** 20 minutes **SERVES:** 4

Creamy Artichoke & Spinach Dip

INGREDIENTS

2 cups baby spinach

1 cup mayonnaise

1 cup shredded parmesan cheese

½ cup chopped artichoke hearts

2 cloves fresh garlic, chopped

½ teaspoon freshly ground black pepper

DIRECTIONS

Preheat the oven to 425°. Mix all the ingredients, and pour into a small ovenproof dish that's large enough to hold about 3 cups of dip. Bake for at least 20 minutes or until bubbly and golden on top and heated through. Serve with warm bread or veggies. Even toasted corn chips are lovely!

Pico de Gallo

PREP TIME: 10 minutes **SERVES:** 4

Pico de Gallo

> I recently attended a great friend's bridal shower. I brought this Pico de Gallo to get the party going, and we couldn't get enough! Some of us were even eating it with our forks; it's that good! Think outside the box when it comes to this recipe. Use it as a topping on fish, steak, or chicken. Bake it on top of salmon. Serve it with chips and margaritas with friends!

INGREDIENTS

- 2 cups quartered cherry tomatoes
- 1 (12-ounce) can diced Mexican-style tomatoes in juice
- ¼ to ½ cup chopped cilantro
- ½ medium red onion, finely diced
- Juice and zest of 2 limes
- 1 tablespoon white vinegar
- 1 clove fresh garlic, smashed and diced with salt to form a paste
- 1 jalapeño pepper, finely diced (use the seeds for a fiery kick, or omit the seeds for a milder bite)
- ¼ teaspoon red pepper flakes
- Salt and pepper to taste

DIRECTIONS

Combine all the ingredients except salt and pepper in a large mixing bowl. Mix, then taste for heat, and add salt and pepper.

I like to let this hang out on the counter for at least 1 hour before I refrigerate it. It gives time for all the lovely flavors to marry. Prepare and use it right away if you need to, or you can make it up to 1 day in advance. I don't use it more than 2 days after it's prepared, as the fresh tomatoes lose a bit of their brightness and taste!

PREP TIME: 5 minutes **COOK TIME:** 20 to 25 minutes **SERVES:** 4

Spicy Baked Hominy

I love Corn Nuts and was trying to make them one day, but all I got were these heavenly, chewy, salty, spicy bits of corn goodness that I ate until they were gone! I imagine they'd be amazing as a topping to salads and soups and even street tacos! Crack a beer, and enjoy this guilt-free snack.

INGREDIENTS

- 1 (15-ounce) can hominy, drained and rinsed
- 2 tablespoons coconut or vegetable oil
- 1 teaspoon freshly ground black pepper
- 1 teaspoon garlic powder
- 1 teaspoon ground paprika
- 1 teaspoon salt

DIRECTIONS

Preheat the oven to 350°. Combine all the ingredients in a bowl. Mix together and pour onto a lined baking sheet; I like to use parchment, but foil works great, too. Bake for 20 to 25 minutes until sizzling and lightly browned. Take care to turn them a few times during cooking.

PREP TIME: 5 minutes **COOK TIME:** 8 to 10 minutes **SERVES:** 4

Brie Bruschetta with Seasonal Fruit

This lovely recipe changes up with seasonal fruit: strawberries, figs, and nectarines are lovely as well. Warm, melted, caramelized Brie pairs beautifully with any stone fruit, pear, or crisp apple!

INGREDIENTS

8 1-inch slices crusty Italian bread
8 ¼-inch slices Brie
2 ripe red, Bosc or Bartlett pears
½ cup toasted walnuts (optional)
Balsamic Reduction (see recipe page 31)

DIRECTIONS

Preheat the oven to 425° (use the convection setting if available). Distribute the Italian bread slices on a cookie sheet, and place one slice of Brie on each. Bake for 8 to 10 minutes, just enough time for the Brie to caramelize. Keep a watchful eye to ensure the Brie is melting properly and forming a golden crust. Remove from the oven, place one slice of pear on each piece, and sprinkle with toasted walnuts. Drizzle with Balsamic Reduction.

PREP TIME: 10 minutes **COOK TIME:** 15 minutes **SERVES:** 4

Rosemary & Bacon Flatbread

> This is by far one of the tastiest flatbread recipes you'll ever taste! It's quick and unique. Bacon makes everything better, but it really is lovely with the chewy flatbread. I like to use naan bread straight on the oven racks.

INGREDIENTS

- 1 cup diced cooked bacon
- ¾ cup shredded parmesan cheese
- ½ cup diced fresh mozzarella
- ¼ cup Signature Citrus Vinaigrette (see recipe page 264)
- 1 teaspoon diced fresh rosemary
- ½ teaspoon freshly cracked black pepper
- 2 to 3 flatbreads

DIRECTIONS

Preheat the oven to 400° on the convection setting, if available. Combine the first six ingredients in a bowl, and spoon a few tablespoons of the mixture onto the flatbread. Bake for 15 minutes or until bubbling and brown; drizzle with a touch more citrus vinaigrette if desired.

PREP TIME: 5 minutes **COOK TIME:** 8 to 10 minutes **SERVES:** 4

Tomato Basil Bruschetta

INGREDIENTS

- 2 12-inch-long Italian-style baguettes, sliced into about 24 ovals
- 1 cup shredded parmesan cheese
- 2 cups diced fresh mozzarella
- 3 cups grape or cherry tomatoes, halved
- 3 teaspoons jarred minced garlic (it offers less of a bite)
- 1 teaspoon sea salt
- 1 teaspoon black pepper
- 12 large, sweet basil leaves, cut in a chiffonade (thin strips)
- ¾ cup good olive oil
- ½ cup aged balsamic vinegar

DIRECTIONS

Preheat the oven to 425°. Slice the bread and arrange on a parchment-lined cookie sheet. Top each slice of bread with both cheeses. Set aside. In a large bowl, in this order, combine halved tomatoes, garlic, salt, pepper, and basil. Mix thoroughly. Be sure to coat each tomato with garlic and seasonings. Taste for salt and pepper. Allow the tomato mixture to stand at room temperature before adding the olive oil. Place the sheet with the cheesy bread in the oven and bake for 1 minutes or until the cheese is bubbling and brown at the edges. (Sometimes I will turn the oven to broil on high for 1 minute to get the nice brown crust on the cheese.) Remove from the oven once the desired crust is reached. Add olive oil to the tomato mixture, and mix thoroughly. Spoon the seasoned tomatoes over the cheesy bread. Drizzle plenty of balsamic vinegar over each bruschetta slice.

Salads & Side Dishes

Play with ingredients, create wonderful flavors, and see what you come up with.

We are only as good as our support systems. Think of these recipes as the support you need to turn your meal into a complete thought!

There are exceptions to every rule, but we generally don't want to eat solely a plate of meat. A nice salad or side of roasted vegetables truly rounds out a meal.

Crisp, crunchy, cool, and creamy: I really love the ways we can describe a salad. A salad doesn't have to contain lettuce every time either: use a nice mix of lentils and fresh citrus or creamy cheese and nuts. Any way I spin it, a salad is invited to almost every meal I make in one way or another.

And what's a great salad without a great dressing? I will never forget when I learned to make dressings from scratch. It was like an entire world opened up to me! I had no idea it was so simple and even healthy to prepare dressings at home. And, just as with the salad itself, dressings have a lot of range in terms of the ingredients you can employ.

I love to think in terms of balance when I'm preparing any meal. Your taste buds tell you whether a food is salty, sweet, sour, bitter, or any combination thereof. If you're thinking in terms of balance, you can achieve greatness every time. Does the dish hit all the notes, and is there any room for improvement? Play with ingredients, create wonderful flavors, and see what you come up with. Great vinaigrettes, for example, have each of these elements, and the dressing you use to complement your fresh mix of ingredients makes all the difference.

PREP TIME: 10 minutes **COOK TIME:** 3 to 5 minutes **SERVES:** 4

Asparagus & Cherry Tomato Panzanella

I love bread salads, and this one is great.
I switch it up by roasting the tomatoes and onions in the fall, but I simply use fresh in the summer when the harvest is going strong!

INGREDIENTS

1 pound asparagus, trimmed
3 cups stale Italian bread, torn into bite-size pieces
2 cups cherry tomatoes, halved
1 cup shaved parmesan cheese
½ red onion, sliced paper-thin into rounds
1 cup basil, torn
1 cup Balsamic Dressing (see recipe below)
1 teaspoon salt
1 teaspoon freshly ground black pepper

DIRECTIONS

Cook the asparagus first: just a big pot of salted boiling water, and in goes the asparagus for 3 to 5 minutes. Then plunge it into ice water to stop the cooking and keep the parts green. Cut the spears into roughly the size of the bread, about 1 to 2 inches. In a large bowl, add all the ingredients. Mix it up; it's that easy.

Balsamic Dressing

½ cup balsamic vinegar
½ cup olive oil
Juice of one lemon
1 clove fresh garlic, crushed
1 teaspoon freshly ground black pepper
1 teaspoon salt

DIRECTIONS

Mix all the ingredients in a bowl.

PREP TIME: 15 minutes **COOK TIME:** 15 minutes **YIELDS:** 12 to 14 biscuits

Black Pepper Buttermilk Biscuits

INGREDIENTS

2 cups flour

2 teaspoons freshly cracked black pepper

1 tablespoon baking powder

½ cup plus 2 tablespoons (10 tablespoons total) cold salted butter

1 cup Bulgarian or full-fat buttermilk

DIRECTIONS

Preheat the oven to 400°. Mix the flour, pepper, and baking powder in a bowl. Cut the butter into the flour using a pastry cutter or two butter knives until it's the size of peas. Add the buttermilk, and mix until the dough begins to come together. If it is too dry, add a splash more buttermilk. Do not overmix, or the light texture of the biscuit will disappear. Turn the dough out onto a floured workspace. Form the dough into a rectangle, handling it as little as possible. The dough should be about 1½ inches thick. Slice the dough into squares, and place each square on a baking sheet. Melt the remaining 2 tablespoons of butter in a small saucepan, and brush the dough with the melted butter. Bake for 12 to 15 minutes or until puffed and golden.

Variations include adding 2 tablespoons fresh chives or ½ cup sharp gruyère cheese to the flour before adding the buttermilk. Coarse rosemary salt is also a beautiful addition to the buttered top before baking!

SALADS & SIDE DISHES

PREP TIME: 10 minutes **SERVES:** 4

Blood Orange, Fennel & Pistachio Salad

I love to eat this salad when it's just beginning to turn into spring, just as the winter is going dormant once again and life springs up! It makes me feel sunny, light, and carefree. If that's at all possible with a salad, it sure is with this one. Grapefruit and tangerines are a great addition to this salad. Be creative!

INGREDIENTS

3 firm, ripe blood oranges
1 young, small bulb fennel, fronds intact
¼ cup crumbled feta
¼ cup cracked, pitted olives
¼ cup toasted pistachio nuts
2 tablespoons olive oil
1 tablespoon champagne vinegar
Sea salt flakes to taste

DIRECTIONS

Slice all the peel and pith off the oranges. (I like to do this very delicately so as not to bruise the flesh or sacrifice too much of the juice.) Lay the slices over a medium platter. Shave the bulb of fennel, and sprinkle in a rustic fashion over the top of the oranges. Sprinkle feta, olives, and pistachios over the salad, then drizzle with olive oil. Splash on a small amount of the champagne vinegar, and top with sea salt.

SALADS & SIDE DISHES

PREP TIME: 5 minutes **COOK TIME:** 10 minutes **SERVES:** 4

Brown Butter Carrots

> I like to peel my carrots, but this is certainly optional! I think it looks beautiful, but either way, these carrots are buttery and perfect every time. I love to use golden carrots or any young, tender, fresh carrot.

INGREDIENTS

2 pounds fresh market carrots, tops intact
4 tablespoons butter
½ cup water
Sprig of fresh thyme
Salt and pepper to taste

DIRECTIONS

Rinse and slice the tops off the carrots, leaving about ¼ inch of green at the top of each. In a large sauté pan, melt the butter. Let it begin to foam and just turn caramel in color over medium-high heat. It's very easy to burn butter when you're attempting to brown it, so be very watchful. Set aside.

Add the carrots to a separate sauté pan with the water, and cook until crisp-tender. When the water has evaporated, drizzle with the brown butter. Turn the carrots, and cook over medium heat for around 10 minutes, until carrots are tender and have picked up some beautiful color. Add the thyme once the carrots are finished, and toss to coat. Try a bit of coarse sea salt and freshly cracked black pepper at the end.

SALADS & SIDE DISHES

Creamy Parmesan Soft Polenta

PREP TIME: 5 minutes **SERVES:** 4

Heirloom Tomatoes with Goat Cheese

INGREDIENTS

3 large heirloom tomatoes, any variety
6 ounces chèvre
1 tablespoon sour cream
1 teaspoon freshly ground black pepper
½ cup fresh herbed oil
½ cup toasted hazelnuts (optional)
Sea salt

DIRECTIONS

Slice the tomatoes about ½-inch thick, and arrange on a serving platter. Whip the chèvre, sour cream, and pepper until smooth and creamy. It will take about 3 minutes. Place a tablespoon of cheese mix on each tomato slice. Drizzle with herbed oil, and sprinkle with toasted hazelnuts. Use a fine pinch of sea salt on each tomato.

PREP TIME: 5 minutes **COOK TIME:** 30 to 40 minutes (if using instant polenta, cook time is roughly 10 to 15 minutes) **SERVES:** 4 to 6

Creamy Parmesan Soft Polenta

INGREDIENTS

5 cups unsalted chicken stock
2 tablespoons olive oil
1 cup medium grind cornmeal
Splash of milk (optional)
1 cup grated parmesan cheese
1 cup heavy cream
3 tablespoons cold butter
Freshly cracked black pepper and sea salt to taste

DIRECTIONS

In a large saucepan, bring chicken stock and olive oil to a simmer. Slowly whisk in the cornmeal and cook over low heat, stirring constantly until mixture begins to thicken (it will take about 30 to 40 minutes to completely cook). If the mixture is too thick, add a splash of stock or milk. Remove from the heat, and add the parmesan cheese, cream, butter, pepper, and salt to taste. Mix well, and serve immediately!

Deconstructed Shrimp Niçoise Platter

PREP TIME: 10 minutes **COOK TIME:** 20 to 25 minutes **SERVES:** 4

Deconstructed Shrimp Niçoise Platter

> Isn't the best part of any salad the toppings? I like crunchy lettuce as much as the next guy, but sometimes I'm in it strictly for the toppings. This is an easy, lovely platter that serves four people happily for a light lunch or as an appetizer before a meal. It's beautiful and social, not to mention impressive! This recipe has several separate cooking instructions for each part of the dish; once everything is cooked, you can assemble!

INGREDIENTS

- 12 slices thick-cut applewood-smoked bacon
- 4 Yukon Gold potatoes
- 1 pound asparagus
- 1 cup cherry tomatoes
- 1 pound large shrimp
- 1 cup Castelvetrano olives (or any olive you prefer)
- 4 6-Minute Eggs, halved (see recipe page 64)
- ½ cup Signature Citrus Vinaigrette (see recipe page 264)

DIRECTIONS

Cook the bacon in a large flat skillet or frying pan at no more than medium heat. This will render the fat nicely to cook the potatoes. Reserve the drippings in the pan. In a large pot of cool water, bring the potatoes to a boil for 10 minutes, until they're al dente. With about 4 minutes to go, drop in the asparagus. (You want it barely cooked with a nice bite; 4 minutes does the trick.) Drain and set the potatoes and asparagus aside. (If you wish, you can pop the asparagus in an ice bath to retain the color, but it's optional.)

Slice the potatoes in ½-inch slices; form one single layer in the pan with the bacon drippings, and cook slowly over medium heat until the potatoes are soft and creamy, about 30 minutes.

Place the tomatoes on a cookie sheet, and put under the broiler on high, with the oven door cracked, for 5 to 6 minutes, watching very carefully. (I love char on the tomatoes, and I let some burst.)

You can steam your own shrimp or purchase them already steamed from your fish counter! To assemble, simply cluster the ingredients on a large platter, and drizzle Signature Citrus Vinaigrette over the entire platter! Serve with warm bread and lots of chilled white wine.

SALADS & SIDE DISHES

6-Minute Egg

For this 6-minute egg, you MUST start with room-temperature eggs. I put on a pot of water to boil with ½ cup white vinegar, and once it's reached a boil, I add room- temperature eggs. I set the timer for 6 minutes, spoon the eggs out, and transfer them immediately to an ice bath to stop cooking. Once they're cool, I give one firm rap at the widest part of the egg, where that little bubble hides, and gently slip the shells off! I can remember my first time doing this: I was too eager, and my poor little eggs looked terrible. Don't be worried if your eggs don't slip out of their shells with ease on your first try. It's a tender little business inside there.

Put an Egg on It!

I feel like every good dish can be made extraordinary by putting a sunny-side, poached, soft-boiled, or hard-cooked egg right on top!

If I had to pick one favorite food, it'd be an egg. Nothing better than the rich yolk atop whole-grain toast, noodles, braises, or by itself. All hail the mighty egg! I especially love a fried egg with a crispy edge and an oozy yolk on a salad.

The true mark of a great cook is how well he or she can cook an egg. You'd be surprised how quickly the gems can become rubbery and overcooked. Medium temperatures and lots of salted butter make for a great egg every time. You can't rush perfection. My two favorite preparations of eggs are a simple 6-Minute Egg (see recipe above) and a sunny-side up fried egg.

Low and slow is the name of the game.

64   SALADS & SIDE DISHES

PREP TIME: 10 minutes **SERVES:** 2

Frisée Salad with Hazelnuts & Crispy Fried Egg

> One of my favorite salads is Frisée with Apple Cider Honey Mustard, toasted hazelnuts, and fresh radishes. I put a lovely, crispy-edged sunny egg on top, and it's perfect!

INGREDIENTS

1 head frisée lettuce
¼ cup toasted hazelnuts
5 to 6 radishes, sliced
1 tablespoon butter
2 eggs
¼ cup Apple Cider Honey Mustard (see recipe page 254)

DIRECTIONS

Clean and chop the frisée lettuce, and arrange on two plates. Evenly sprinkle the hazelnuts and radishes over the lettuce. In a medium nonstick skillet, melt the butter over medium-high heat, and let it get bubbly (careful not to burn). Crack the eggs, and fry them in the hot butter. After about 2 minutes, place the lid over the pan, and let the tops of the eggs steam slightly (this is how I get rid of the raw texture in a sunny-side up egg). Continue to cook the eggs with the lid off for another 2 to 3 minutes, until the edges are golden and crisp. Place one egg on each salad, and drizzle with honey mustard! This is such an easy light lunch or appetizer salad before dinner.

PREP TIME: 5 minutes **COOK TIME:** 5 minutes **SERVES:** 4

Herbed Couscous with Avocado & Slivered Almonds

INGREDIENTS

2 cups chicken stock

1 teaspoon salt

1 cup dry, plain couscous

3 green onions, sliced

½ cup toasted, slivered almonds

2 Roma tomatoes, diced

3 tablespoons chopped fresh flat-leaf parsley

½ cup Signature Citrus Vinaigrette (see recipe page 264)

1 avocado, sliced

1 tablespoon fresh lemon juice

DIRECTIONS

Bring the stock and salt to a simmer. Add the couscous and stir. Remove from the heat, and let stand covered for 5 minutes. Fluff with a fork, cover, and let stand another 5 minutes.

Turn out the couscous into a large mixing bowl, and add the green onions, almonds, tomatoes, parsley, and vinaigrette. Gently use two large serving spoons or forks to mix. In a separate small dish, pour the lemon juice over the sliced avocado to keep its green color, and mix into the couscous. This will keep for up to 1 day. If you're making the couscous in advance, just add the avocado right before you serve it!

PREP TIME: 10 minutes **SERVES:** 4 to 6

Cilantro Cabbage Slaw

INGREDIENTS

1 small head Napa cabbage

1 sweet carrot, shredded or grated (about 1 cup)

1 bunch of cilantro, diced (about ¾ cup loosely packed)

1 jalapeño, diced

¼ cup lime juice

2 tablespoons apple cider vinegar

1 tablespoon honey

1 teaspoon freshly ground black pepper

1 teaspoon red chili flakes

1 teaspoon salt

¾ cup canola oil

DIRECTIONS

Prepare the cabbage by slicing it in half lengthwise and rinsing thoroughly under cold water, taking care to remove any sand or dirt from the leaves. Drain and slice very thick, long slices, almost shredding the cabbage. Place the sliced cabbage in a large mixing bowl. Add the carrots, cilantro, and jalapeño. (Remove the pepper's ribs and seeds if you want less of a spicy kick.) Dress the salad with all remaining ingredients except the oil in a separate bowl. Mix using a light hand and tongs so you don't destroy the cabbage. Once the slaw is mixed, dress with canola oil. Mix lightly to combine again, using tongs. Taste for seasoning. Allow the mixture to stand for at least 30 minutes before serving. The acid from the lime juice will wilt the cabbage slightly and make it very tasty!

SALADS & SIDE DISHES

PREP TIME: 5 minutes **SERVES:** 4

Lentils & Jicama

INGREDIENTS

1 cup thinly sliced jicama

1 cup spinach

½ cup diced tomato

¼ cup chopped chives

¼ cup thinly sliced red onion

3 tablespoons olive oil

2 tablespoons lemon juice

1 tablespoon Thai chili paste

1 teaspoon crushed garlic

1 teaspoon freshly ground black pepper

1 teaspoon salt

1 (15-ounce) can lentils, rinsed

¼ cup crumbled feta

DIRECTIONS

In a mixing bowl, gently mix all the ingredients except the lentils and feta. Gently fold the lentils into the dressing, and top with crumbled feta! This is my favorite easy side dish for any fish.

PREP TIME: 10 to 12 minutes **SERVES:** 4

Orzo with Dill & Tomatoes

Simple tastes good.
Ha! I used to find myself poring over crazy combinations of food trying to be new and different. Long gone are those days. Now I just focus on freshness and flavor. Life got so much easier when I stopped trying to keep up and started living, particularly with what's in our fridge on any given day.

INGREDIENTS

- 1 (8-ounce) box orzo pasta, cooked (about 3 cups)
- ½ cup chopped fresh dill (do not use dry)
- 1½ cups shredded parmesan cheese
- 1 cup halved cherry tomatoes
- ½ cup olive oil
- 1 teaspoon salt
- 1 teaspoon freshly ground black pepper
- Juice and zest from 1 lemon

DIRECTIONS

Add the cooked, drained orzo to a large mixing bowl, and add the dill, cheese, and tomatoes. (I never mind if the orzo is still warm, but I do rinse it for a minute in cool water.) Gently whisk the olive oil, salt, pepper, lemon juice, and zest together in a separate bowl. Pour evenly over the salad, and toss! It's really that simple. Add grilled shrimp or fish, and you've got dinner instead of a side!

PREP TIME: 10 to 15 minutes **ROAST TIME:** 15 to 20 minutes **SERVES:** 4

Parchment Paper Vegetables

There is nothing quite as simple or stunning to serve as a gorgeous pouch of oven-steamed veggies dripping with olive oil, fresh herbs, and a drizzle of fresh lemon or balsamic vinegar. It's truly the perfect side to any dinner. You can add or take away any veggie combo; in fact, asparagus and sweet pea pods are wonderful as well!

INGREDIENTS

4 young spring carrots
4 golden or purple beets
4 spring onions
4 cloves garlic
4 12-inch by 12-inch sheets of parchment paper
4 tablespoons olive oil
Salt and pepper
Fresh dill or fresh lemon thyme
Lemon juice or balsamic vinegar

DIRECTIONS

Preheat the oven to 425°. Wash and prep the spring veggies. (I like to thinly slice the beets and cut the carrots lengthwise, keeping everything about the same size or width.) To assemble each pouch, place the veggies in the center of one piece of parchment paper, drizzle with olive, sprinkle with salt and pepper, and add sprigs of fresh herbs. Fold the paper in half on itself, then start at the corner and fold over the edges to create a true pouch. Set on a cookie sheet, and repeat the process for the next pouches. Place the baking sheet with the pouches into the oven for 15 to 20 minutes. They will be perfectly cooked and full of flavor. When you serve, have guests tear open the pouch and squeeze lemon or drizzle balsamic vinegar on the vegetables.

PREP TIME: 10 to 15 minutes **SERVES:** 4

Red Quinoa with Chèvre & Arugula

INGREDIENTS

3 cups red quinoa (cooked according to package directions in stock, not water)

¾ cup crumbled chèvre or any sharp goat cheese

1 cup toasted walnuts

1 cup Signature Citrus Vinaigrette (see recipe page 264)

1 cup halved cherry tomatoes

2 cups baby arugula

Salt and pepper to taste

DIRECTIONS

In a large mixing bowl, add all the ingredients in the order they're listed. Gently mix the contents, and let stand 10 to 15 minutes for all the flavors to marry. This tastes even better after it's been in the fridge overnight!

PREP TIME: 10 minutes **BAKE TIME:** 30 minutes **SERVES:** 4

Roasted Delicata Squash with Garlic

INGREDIENTS

2 delicata squash
1 teaspoon salt
1 teaspoon freshly ground black pepper
10 cloves fresh garlic, peeled
2 to 3 tablespoons chopped fresh basil
2 to 3 tablespoons olive oil
Feta cheese, fresh basil, and toasted walnuts as garnish (optional)

DIRECTIONS

Preheat the oven to 350°. Slice the delicata squash in half, and scoop out the seeds. Slice the squash in ¾-inch slices crosswise to make them half-moon shaped. Place the slices in a large mixing bowl, and add salt, pepper, garlic, basil, and oil. Toss to coat everything evenly, then pour onto a cookie sheet and bake for at least 30 minutes. You can eat the skin on a young delicata squash, and it tastes great!

This is such a simple dish and looks great for entertaining. Sprinkle with feta and toasted walnuts. The garlic gets crispy and sweet and is a great little beer snack.

PREP TIME: 5 minutes **BAKE TIME:** 30 minutes **YIELDS:** one 9×13-inch baking pan or 12 to 16 muffins

Garlic & Cheddar Corn Bread

> *Probably the most flavorful corn bread you may ever taste.*
> This recipe makes a surprisingly moist and beautiful batch of corn bread that'll have you making it for every gathering! If you find that the crunchy texture of medium stone-ground cornmeal is too much, you can use a finer mill, or soak your cornmeal in the milk and vinegar for up to 2 hours, then add another ¾ cup of milk.

INGREDIENTS

- ½ cup butter
- ½ cup olive oil
- 1 cup sugar
- 4 eggs
- 1 teaspoon salt
- 1 tablespoon champagne or white vinegar
- 2 cups whole milk
- 2 cups medium stone-ground cornmeal
- 2 cups flour
- 4 teaspoons baking powder
- 2 cups shredded cheddar cheese
- 2 cloves fresh garlic, crushed

DIRECTIONS

Preheat the oven to 350°, and liberally butter a 9×13-inch baking pan or muffin cups. Melt the butter in a large mixing bowl, and add the ingredients in the order they are listed. Don't overmix. Pour into the pan or muffin cups, and bake for 30 minutes or until a toothpick comes out clean when inserted into the center of the corn bread.

Whole-Grain Mustard/Shallot Vinaigrette Potatoes

PREP TIME: 5 minutes **COOK TIME:** 40 to 60 minutes **SERVES:** 4

Whole-Grain Mustard/Shallot Vinaigrette Potatoes

INGREDIENTS

6 to 7 medium Yukon Gold potatoes
1 cup good olive oil
¼ cup diced shallots
¼ cup fresh lemon juice
¼ cup whole-grain mustard
2 tablespoons brown mustard
1 teaspoon freshly cracked black pepper
1 teaspoon kosher salt
¼ teaspoon onion powder
½ cup chopped fresh parsley for garnish

DIRECTIONS

Start by boiling the potatoes. For perfect boiled potatoes, place them in a pot and cover with room-temperature or cool water, not cold. Bring to a boil over high heat, then reduce heat to medium and cover for 40 to 60 minutes. Drain, and allow enough time to cool so the skins peel right off. This yields a creamy potato EVERY time.

Next, mix all the ingredients for the vinaigrette, and drizzle over the potatoes. Sprinkle the parsley over the top, and serve at room temperature or after chilling. Any way you slice it, this stuff is amazing!

PREP TIME: 5 minutes **COOK TIME:** 60 minutes **SERVES:** 4

Rosemary & Tomato White Beans

Let's be very real for a moment: I thought I invented cassoulet. Don't laugh at me or judge me too harshly. Mine is a variation from a traditional cassoulet and can be vegetarian if needed! I prefer the richness chicken stock adds. These beautiful beans make a great side dish for fish or any grilled meat.

INGREDIENTS

1 medium white onion, diced
2 tablespoons olive oil
3 cloves fresh garlic, minced
1 sprig fresh rosemary
2 (15-ounce) cans cannellini beans, drained and rinsed
1 cup white wine
½ cup water or chicken stock
4 Roma tomatoes, diced
1 teaspoon salt
1 teaspoon freshly ground black pepper
2 tablespoons butter
Squeeze of fresh lemon juice

DIRECTIONS

Cook the onions in the olive oil in a medium saucepan until the onions become soft, about 5 minutes. Add the garlic and rosemary, and cook about 1 minute, until the mixture becomes fragrant. Add the beans, wine, water or stock, tomatoes, and salt and pepper. Simmer the whole mixture over medium-low heat until the beans are creamy and tender, about 1 hour. When it's finished and thick (the beans will have kept their shape), add the butter and a squeeze of fresh lemon. Remove the sprig of rosemary.

SALADS & SIDE DISHES

Roasted Yukon Golds with Asparagus & Rosemary

PREP TIME: 10 minutes **ROAST TIME:** 30 to 40 minutes **SERVES:** 4

Roasted Yukon Golds with Asparagus & Rosemary

Crispy, creamy potatoes are amazing with crispy, chewy roasted asparagus. This is the perfect side dish or party snack for anyone who breathes! The potatoes get a crisp crust and stay tender on the inside, and who can resist garlicky dipping sauce?

INGREDIENTS

- 4–5 medium Yukon Gold potatoes
- ½ pound asparagus spears, trimmed
- 6 tablespoons olive oil
- 3 sprigs fresh rosemary
- 1 teaspoon freshly ground black pepper
- 1 teaspoon salt
- 1 cup Herbed Aioli (see recipe page 262)

DIRECTIONS

Preheat oven to 375°, scrub the potatoes, and pat dry. Slice each potato into wedges by slicing in half lengthwise and then again into at least 6 to 8 sections per potato. Place in a large mixing bowl. Add asparagus, oil, rosemary, salt, and pepper, and mix, making sure to coat every veggie with oil and seasonings. Pour onto a large cookie sheet, making sure to have only a single layer. Otherwise, you won't get crisp veggies; you'll get steamed, soggy veggies. Roast for 30 to 40 minutes, rotating the pan once about halfway through. When the potatoes are tender in the center with a golden color, they are finished. I always let the potatoes cool for about 10 minutes on the cookie sheet to regain a bit of their creamy texture. Serve with chilled Herbed Aioli.

Watermelon Salad with Feta & Cilantro

PREP TIME: 10 minutes **SERVES:** 4

Strawberry & Goat Cheese Salad

INGREDIENTS

2 cups sliced strawberries
½ cup crumbled goat cheese
½ cup toasted pecan halves
¼ cup Balsamic Reduction (see recipe page 31)

DIRECTIONS

If you like, you will get 4 small salads, a perfect start to any meal. Feel free to assemble on four small plates or one larger platter. Add ¼ of berries to each plate, sprinkle cheese and nuts over, and drizzle with Balsamic Reduction!

PREP TIME: 10 minutes **SERVES:** 4

Watermelon Salad with Feta & Cilantro

[This is so pretty served family-style.

INGREDIENTS

3 cups ripe seedless watermelon, cubed
¼ cup crumbled feta
½ cup chopped cilantro
½ cup prepared Lime Cilantro Dressing (see recipe page 267)
¼ teaspoon freshly cracked black pepper

DIRECTIONS

Add cubed watermelon to a large, shallow serving bowl or dish, and sprinkle with feta and cilantro. Lightly pour dressing over the top, and finish with cracked black pepper. Do not toss or mix. Simply serve as a starter to your meal or as a light lunch.

Soup's On

Sometimes in life, it's important that we move against the grain.

I was once fired from the banking world. Too many missed facts and important duties I just couldn't seem to hack. I called up a dear friend who owned a little wine bar. "I need a job. I've got nothing," I told her. I was twenty-two with a house payment and big responsibilities. She told me she could use my help serving.

The job was difficult for me, waiting tables, remembering customers' orders, and trying to do it with style and grace. About a year into working there, I had become quite the jack-of-all-trades, helping in the kitchen and wheeling that mop bucket with flair. I was still so awkward in life. I had no idea what I was doing or where I was going, but every time I got the opportunity to cook, I'd come alive.

The act of cooking was exciting and fun, and all of a sudden, my problems seemed smaller and my stress would lift. This would happen especially when making soup. For years before I started cooking, I had a notebook detailing foods I'd love to serve at my own restaurant, which was merely imaginary at the time. I spent so much time daydreaming about where it would be located, the ambiance, the sophisticated yet playful wine list I'd curate.

Meanwhile, the owners of the wine bar were leaving for vacation, and they left the place in the charge of some good friends. I had been begging to add soup to the menu for a few months. We weren't set up to serve soup, but pushing the envelope has always been my forte. Since the wine bar's cook often dreamt up wonderful specials the customers greatly enjoyed, I figured I'd take the occasion of my employer's absence to conjure up one of my own.

I'd made this butternut squash soup in my home kitchen several times. It was wonderful, so unique and different. Whenever I'd ask if we could try to sell it, the answer was always "maybe one day." When they left on vacation, I asked the cook if we could try it, and she said, "Why not!" I made my soup, eager for the customers to try it. We sold through the entire pot, yielding a $90 profit. I could barely contain my excitement when it came time to regale the owners with the tale of my rock star butternut squash soup!

While the owners were happy the dish was a success with customers, they weren't exactly pleased with my breaking the rules. The soup, while incredible, wasn't cleared with the health department. I grudgingly made my apology and understood that it may not have been the wisest choice for the wine bar, but hey, I knew I had to try.

Something clicked deep inside me. It would be several years before I opened my own restaurant, but the fire was lit. Watching the way people responded to my cooking was life-giving. I walked out of the kitchen with this sense of joy and excitement. The customers were so delighted. My soup, they said, tasted different from anything they'd tried and was simply wonderful.

This response made an impact on me and taught me that sometimes in life, it's important that we move against the grain. It can be uncomfortable and poorly received, to be certain, but it has the power and ability to change our course. I'll be forever grateful for the experiences I gained and the way I began to uncover what made me tick. If not for this soup and bending the rules, who knows if I would have been able to venture out into the food world. I had no idea what was to come. God had planted this tiny seed. The oak tree was beginning its story, and there would doubtless be storms for it to weather. But oak trees bend and persevere, year after year.

I am grateful for this soup. It changed my life, and I hope the ritual of making a pot of hot, comforting soup to share with your loved ones changes yours.

Beef Barcelona Stew

PREP TIME: 10 minutes **BRAISE TIME:** 3 hours **SERVES:** 4 to 6

Beef Barcelona Stew

> *This is definitely beef stew with an attitude,* and it's the ultimate comfort on a chilly day.

INGREDIENTS

- 1½ pounds stewing beef (any tough, marbled cut will do)
- 1 cup all-purpose flour
- 2 teaspoons freshly ground black pepper
- 3 teaspoons kosher salt
- 4 cups beef stock
- 3 Yukon Gold potatoes, chopped
- 2 cups chopped collard greens
- 2 cups chopped Roma tomatoes
- 2 carrots, sliced
- 1 green pepper, chopped
- 1 red pepper, chopped
- 1 onion, chopped
- 1 small sweet potato, cubed
- 3 tablespoons butter
- 3 tablespoons double concentrated tomato paste
- 3 cloves fresh garlic, crushed
- 2 tablespoons ground paprika
- 1 teaspoon dried Mexican oregano
- 1 teaspoon ground cayenne pepper
- 1 teaspoon ground smoked paprika

DIRECTIONS

Preheat the oven to 350°. Place the meat in a large ziplock bag, and toss with the flour. Dust off the excess flour, and brown meat in the same ovenproof pot you plan to use for the stew. I recommend an enamel-coated Dutch oven. Liberally salt and pepper the meat as you go. Feel free to do this in batches, so you get a crust on your meat rather than a gray steamed mess. Once the meat is browned, combine everything else in that same pan, and bake for at least 3 hours. When the liquid hits the pot, use a wooden spoon to loosen the browned bits on the bottom of your pan. It's just a lovely stew. We eat this over rice, by itself, or served with warm pita bread for dipping.

PREP TIME: 10 minutes **COOK TIME:** 60 minutes **SERVES:** 4

Chicken Sausage Sweet Potato Stew

INGREDIENTS

- 1 pound mild chicken sausage, out of the casing
- 2 tablespoons olive oil
- 2 white-fleshed sweet potatoes, diced
- 1 medium yellow onion, diced
- 2 carrots, sliced
- 1 tablespoon kosher salt
- ½ teaspoon freshly ground black pepper
- ¼ teaspoon crushed red pepper flakes
- 2 cloves fresh garlic, crushed
- 1 (15-ounce) can diced tomatoes
- 4 cups unsalted chicken stock

DIRECTIONS

Brown the meat in the olive oil in a large soup pot over medium-high heat. Once the meat is cooked, add the sweet potatoes through to the red pepper flakes. Cook for about 3 or 4 minutes. Add the garlic, then the tomatoes and stock. Bring to a boil, then reduce heat to medium-low for 1 hour or until the potatoes are fork-tender.

PREP TIME: 15 to 20 minutes **COOK TIME:** 3 hours **SERVES:** 4

Beef Bourguignon

INGREDIENTS

- 3 teaspoons kosher salt, divided
- 2 teaspoons pepper, divided
- 1 cup all-purpose flour (for dredging)
- 2 pounds beef, cubed (chuck is best)
- 3 tablespoons butter
- 2 tablespoons olive oil
- 4 to 6 red potatoes, skin on, quartered or smaller, depending on size
- 3 to 4 Roma tomatoes, cut into quarters
- 2 leeks, cleaned and sliced into quarters
- 2 cups bias-cut carrots
- 2 cups bias-cut parsnips
- 1 medium yellow onion, halved and sliced
- 4 cloves fresh garlic, chopped
- 1 (750-milliliter) bottle pinot noir or French blend wine (you want a light, juicy red)
- 2 cups unsalted beef stock
- 2 sprigs fresh thyme
- 2 sprigs fresh rosemary
- Diced fresh parsley to finish

DIRECTIONS

Preheat the oven to 350°. Add 1 teaspoon salt, 1 teaspoon pepper, and the flour to a brown paper bag. Add the meat, and shake the bag to coat evenly. Dust the excess flour off the meat. Melt the butter and olive oil in a large, enamel-coated Dutch oven over medium-high heat. Add the dredged meat, and brown on all sides, about 10 minutes. Do not overcrowd your pan, or you will have gray meat; you're looking for golden brown, not cooked. (You could brown the meat in two batches.) Once the meat is browned, remove it from the pan and set aside. Add potatoes through onion to the pan. Cook for about 5 minutes over medium heat, add the garlic, and cook for 1 additional minute. Deglaze the pan with the entire bottle of wine. Add the meat back in, and make sure to loosen the brown bits off the bottom with a wooden spoon. Add beef stock, herbs, and remaining salt and pepper. Place the pot, covered, into the oven for 3 hours. Garnish with fresh parsley, and serve with warm, crusty bread and butter.

PREP TIME: 60 minutes **COOK TIME:** 30 minutes **SERVES:** 4

Butternut Squash Soup

INGREDIENTS

2 medium butternut squash

6 tablespoons olive oil, divided

Salt and pepper to taste

1 medium yellow onion, diced

1 cup chopped carrots

1 cup white wine

6 cups chicken stock

1 cup heavy cream

Parmesan cheese, sliced green onions, and croutons, to top (optional)

DIRECTIONS

Preheat oven to 400°. Slice butternut squash lengthwise, discarding the seeds and pulp. Rub the exposed flesh side with 1 tablespoon of olive oil, and sprinkle with salt and pepper. Place skin side up on a cookie sheet, cover the squash with foil, and roast for 60 minutes or until flesh is tender and skin is easily removed with spoon. In a large, heavy-bottomed soup pot, sauté onion and carrots until tender in the remaining 5 tablespoons of olive oil. Salt and pepper this step, too. Once the veggies are tender and have a bit of color, add the wine, and simmer for 3 to 4 minutes. Using a wooden spoon, make sure to get any browned bits off the bottom of the pan. Add the roasted flesh of the butternut squash and chicken stock; simmer for 30 minutes. Remove from heat. Using an immersion stick blender, blend the hot soup until smooth (soup will be slightly thickened). Add cream. Serve immediately with sprinkles of parmesan cheese and green onions or homemade buttery croutons. Dietary restrictions and food sensitivities aside, none of those ever hurt anyone!

Creamy Tomato Soup

PREP TIME: 10 minutes **COOK TIME:** 60 minutes **SERVES:** 4

Creamy Tomato Soup

> *Warm, comforting one-pot wonder!*
> My family enjoys this soup with a grilled-cheese sammie most of the chilly months firstly for its taste, and secondly for its ease.

INGREDIENTS

1 large yellow onion, chopped
2 large carrots, chopped
1 rib celery, chopped
5 to 7 cloves of fresh garlic, chopped
3 teaspoons salt
1 teaspoon freshly ground black pepper
¼ teaspoon red pepper flakes (or more for extra heat)
¼ cup extra virgin olive oil
2 tablespoons butter
5 cups unsalted chicken stock
2 (15-ounce) cans whole peeled plum tomatoes, in juice or sauce
1 cup heavy cream
1 cup chopped fresh sweet basil

DIRECTIONS

In a large, heavy-bottomed soup or stockpot, add onion, carrots, celery, garlic, and spices to the oil and butter. Sauté over medium heat for about 5 or 6 minutes, until veggies begin to soften. Add stock and tomatoes, juice and all. Simmer all together for about 1 hour over medium heat. Once all the veggies are fall-apart tender, use an immersion blender to puree the entire pot of soup. It should blend up beautifully. Remove the soup from the heat, and add the heavy cream and fresh basil. Taste for salt and pepper!

PREP TIME: 15 minutes **COOK TIME:** 60 minutes to 2 hours **SERVES:** 4

French Onion Soup

INGREDIENTS

1 medium baguette
8 medium Spanish or yellow onions
3 tablespoons butter
5 tablespoons olive oil
3 cloves fresh garlic, crushed
2 cups white wine
½ cup tawny port
2 tablespoons kosher salt
2 teaspoons freshly ground black pepper
6 cups unsalted beef stock
2 sprigs fresh thyme
8 pieces French or Italian bread
8 slices Havarti cheese
1½ cups grated parmesan cheese

DIRECTIONS

Toast one-inch-thick baguette slices in a 425° oven for 4 minutes. Set aside. Thinly slice the onions. In a large stockpot, melt the butter and olive oil together. Add the onions, and caramelize over medium-high heat, about 15 minutes. When the onions have caramelized, add the garlic, and stir for one minute. Add the wine and port to deglaze the pan, and cook for 2 to 3 minutes to soften the flavor of the alcohol. Add salt and pepper. Slowly add the beef stock. Reduce heat to medium-low, add the thyme, and simmer for at least 1 hour (2 hours is perfect!). Ladle the hot soup into 4 to 8 ovenproof vessels (depending on size of the vessels). Top with baguette slices, cover with 1 slice of Havarti and some parmesan, and melt under the broiler setting of the oven, with the door cracked, for 2 to 3 minutes. Be very careful, as the broiler setting can burn the cheese quickly! Watch this step closely. Enjoy with mixed greens on the side.

Pico de Gallo Cioppino

PREP TIME: 30 minutes **COOK TIME:** 15 to 20 minutes **SERVES:** 4

Pico de Gallo Cioppino

INGREDIENTS

2 pounds small littleneck steamer clams, live

½ cup all-purpose flour

2 pounds rockfish, snapper, or other firm-fleshed white fish

1 pound shrimp, tail on

1 small white onion, diced

3 tablespoons olive oil

1 medium jalapeño, diced (include ribs for extra heat)

1 teaspoon red pepper flakes

2 teaspoons salt (or more to taste)

1 teaspoon freshly ground black pepper

4 cloves fresh garlic, crushed

2 cups diced fresh tomatoes

1 (15-ounce) can petite-diced tomatoes in juice

1 cup white wine

2 cups unsalted chicken stock

¾ cup chopped cilantro

2 to 3 limes

DIRECTIONS

Soak live clams in a sink of ice water with flour for 30 minutes before use. The little clams will take in the freshwater; spit out impurities such as sand, dirt, and grit; and ingest the flour. Rinse and drain clams, and set aside in a colander. Cube fish into 2-inch pieces, and set aside with clams and shrimp.

Sweat diced onions in the olive oil over medium-high heat until tender. Add the jalapeño, red pepper flakes, salt, and pepper. Once the veggies are tender, about 6 minutes, add the garlic and sweat for another 30 to 45 seconds. Make sure you don't burn the garlic, or it will taste bitter. Add the fresh and canned tomatoes and their juice, wine, and stock, bringing to a rolling boil. Taste for salt and pepper.

After mixture has boiled for 3 minutes, add the clams, fish, and shrimp. Reduce heat to low, and simmer for 4 to 6 minutes, until the clams open, the shrimp are pink, and the fish is opaque and firm. (If any clams do not open, throw them out and don't eat them!) When the soup is cooked, add the cilantro and juice of 1 lime. Serve with crusty bread or tortilla chips for dipping! Add a few fresh lime slices to each bowl.

Roasted Tomatillo Chile Verde

PREP TIME: 20 minutes **COOK TIME:** 30 minutes **SERVES:** 4

Roasted Tomatillo Chile Verde

INGREDIENTS

- 10 tomatillos
- 2 jalapeños
- 1 onion, diced
- 1 green pepper, diced
- 3 cloves fresh garlic, chopped
- 3 teaspoons kosher salt
- 2 teaspoons dried Mexican oregano
- 2 teaspoons freshly ground black pepper
- 1 teaspoon ground cumin
- 1 teaspoon red pepper flakes
- 3 cups unsalted or low-sodium chicken stock
- 2 (15-ounce) cans cannellini beans, drained and rinsed
- ½ cup chopped cilantro

DIRECTIONS

To roast tomatillos, peel the paper skins away from the flesh of the fruit, and rinse. Arrange fruit on a baking sheet with the jalapeños, and roast at 425° for 15 to 20 minutes. (You're looking for the tomatillos to burst, with a nice amount of browning.) Once finished, remove the sheet from the oven, and set aside to cool.

In a stovetop soup pot, sweat the onion, pepper, garlic, and spices in the olive oil over medium-high heat. Once the veggies are tender (5 to 7 minutes), chop the cooled tomatillos and jalapeños, and add to the pot. Cook over medium heat until thickened slightly, about 10 minutes. Add stock and drained beans. Simmer together, uncovered, for 20 to 30 minutes. Serve garnished with cilantro and accompanied by Garlic & Cheddar Corn Bread (see recipe page 81).

To make this dish even heartier, add shredded rotisserie chicken or one you've roasted yourself at the same time as the beans!

PREP TIME: 10 minutes **COOK TIME:** 60 minutes **SERVES:** 4

Sister's Turkey Minestrone

INGREDIENTS

1 pound lean ground turkey
4 tablespoons olive oil
3 large carrots, diced
3 ribs celery, diced
1 medium yellow onion, diced
1 medium zucchini, diced
2 cloves fresh garlic, crushed
1 tablespoon salt
2 teaspoons dried basil
2 teaspoons freshly ground black pepper
1 teaspoon granulated garlic
6 cups unsalted beef stock
2 cups water
1 (15-ounce) can cannellini beans, drained
1 (15-ounce) can kidney beans, drained
2 (15-ounce) cans diced tomatoes
2 cups dry ditalini pasta
Pecorino Romano or parmesan cheese to garnish (optional)

DIRECTIONS

In a large saucepan, brown the turkey in olive oil until completely cooked; set aside. Add all diced veggies into the same pot, and cook until just tender. Add fresh garlic; stir in for about 1 minute. Add the seasonings, stock, water, beans, and tomatoes. Simmer for 1 hour. In a separate pot, boil the noodles until just before al dente. Add the cooked pasta to the soup about 10 minutes before you're ready to serve the dish.

Top with grated Pecorino Romano or parmesan if you wish.

PREP TIME: 10 minutes **COOK TIME:** 60 minutes **SERVES:** 4

White Bean, Sausage & Spinach Soup

> I love soup, and this has to be one of the easiest yet most impressive soups I've made. When you wait until the last moment to add the lemon juice and spinach, everything in the dish stays vibrant and inviting.

INGREDIENTS

- 16 ounces fresh sweet or hot Italian sausage (your preference), removed from casings
- 1 yellow onion, diced
- 2 tablespoons olive oil
- 4 cloves fresh garlic, chopped
- 1 cup diced carrots
- 1 rib celery, diced
- 2 medium white potatoes, diced
- ½ tablespoon kosher salt
- 1 teaspoon freshly ground black pepper
- 5 cups unsalted chicken stock
- 1 (15-ounce) can white beans, drained and rinsed
- 4 to 5 cups baby spinach
- 2 tablespoons freshly squeezed lemon juice

DIRECTIONS

Brown sausage over medium to medium-high heat in a large stock or soup pot. When sausage is cooked, remove from pot. Add onion and olive oil; sweat until translucent. Add garlic, carrots, celery, potatoes, salt, and pepper. After a few minutes, add the chicken stock, meat, and drippings back to pot. Bring to a simmer for 30 minutes, until veggies are soft. Add white beans, and cook an additional 30 minutes. At the final moment before serving, add spinach and lemon juice. Serve with crusty bread and butter.

The Main Dish

Each night when I showed up to an empty restaurant to start cooking, something came alive in me.

The busiest nights at Minoela were a sight to behold. The turn-of-the-twentieth-century building we resided in was lined with old, single-paned windows that would fog over when we were packed. Wine bottle corks were often strewn about the bar top. The wait staff wove in and out of the makeshift kitchen, bussing, scraping dishes for the dishwasher, and even checking the ovens to see if their orders were up. We only had fourteen tables, including the bar windows and communal table. There were fifteen items on the menu at any given time and at least fifteen items that were not officially on the menu, just an ever-shifting lineup of unique creations—whatever was fresh at the market or needed to get used up from the fridge. People would make their way to the bar counter and get on the list for a table. There was no real semblance of organization, but the whole place smelled like heaven. We were pumping out magic in that kitchen, off of tiny induction burners.

I hired a chef who changed the way I did everything. He had this slow, methodical, sharp mind and was blown away at the quality of ingredients we stocked. Nothing artificial. Fresh herbs and bundles of farmers' market vegetables. At that time in Tacoma, Washington, our restaurant was a bit of a unicorn. No one else in town offered scratch-made anything or served roasted packets of parchment veggies made in tabletop convection ovens. What we lacked in organization we made up for in flavor and spirit.

Our unassuming, piecemeal kitchen wasn't necessarily where one might expect to taste the best food in town. But each night when I showed up to an empty restaurant to start cooking, something came alive in me. Friends would come in, and I'd serve them course after course that were simple and wild at the same time. One of my favorite things to do was roasting beets, dousing them in olive oil and lemon zest, and serving them with crusty fresh bread to sop up the drippings. People said that our pastas, toothsome and full of flavor, reminded them of Italy. I had no idea how special it was; it was just what felt right to us.

I never wore a chef's coat, just a black, slub knit, V-neck T-shirt. I didn't want anyone to know I was the restaurant owner. I'd take messages for people and let them know I'd pass along the info. I didn't care about the prestige of being in charge or anything that went along with that. I just wanted to cook.

We'd serve big piles of greens with shaved parmesan and potatoes crisped to perfection, or Dungeness crab and lemon cream pasta. There were always pestos, heavy with olive oil, sun-dried tomatoes, and fresh ciabatta bread. It was peasant food at its finest. We had no deep fryer, so we'd roast a big sheet of wedged potatoes to be served with parmesan aioli, and since it took a solid forty-five minutes to prepare a new sheet once the last round was depleted, there existed the possibility that the potatoes might not make it onto a guest's order. So popular were the potatoes that guests would ask about them, then take a short stroll before ordering, just to get the timing right. We did everything unconventionally.

Minoela wasn't located in the prettiest part of town, but it was ours, and we cared about every detail. It didn't matter how many or how quickly order tickets stacked up. Each and every dish was cared for. We'd watch closely for the brown bits to appear on the bottoms of the stainless steel pans. Once the fond appeared, then and only then could we grace the pan with cream and gently cooked, fresh handmade fettuccine. I still feel this way today, cooking for my family. At the restaurant, I learned how important waiting can be, and how the details accumulate to make something greater than themselves.

When you are cooking dinner from now on, take the browning on all the meats, onions, and herbs just a touch further; it's where the magic happens. Add an extra splash of olive oil and a dusting of flaky sea salt. Enjoy your food more. Don't overindulge exactly… just prepare what you are cooking with a bit more love.

PREP TIME: 25 to 30 minutes **COOK TIME:** 15 minutes **SERVES:** 4

Angel Hair Pasta with Roasted Summer Veggies

> The trick to perfect roasted or baked veggies is to avoid overcrowding your pan and to choose veggies that are around the same size and texture. I wouldn't roast potatoes with a pepper, for example, because the peppers might burn by the time the harder root veggies are finished.

INGREDIENTS

2 zucchini
1 red bell pepper
1 yellow onion
1 yellow squash
½ cup olive oil, divided
2 teaspoons freshly ground black pepper, divided
2 teaspoons salt, divided, plus more for boiling water
3 anchovy fillets
1 (16-ounce) can diced tomatoes in juice (not sauce)
3 cloves garlic
½ teaspoon red chili flakes
½ pound angel hair pasta, cooked not quite al dente
1 cup pasta water, reserved
½ cup chopped fresh parsley

DIRECTIONS

Preheat the oven to 400°. Slice the veggies roughly the same size, about ⅛-inch thick. Reserve half the onion slices. Place the sliced veggies on a cookie sheet, and drizzle with 2 tablespoons olive oil, 1 teaspoon pepper, and 1 teaspoon salt. Roast for 25 to 30 minutes until veggies are soft and caramelized. Set aside.

Sauté the reserved onion slices in the remaining oil in a large frying pan over medium heat until soft and translucent. Add the anchovy fillets, and cook until anchovies are fragrant and completely dissolved into the onions. Turn heat up to medium-high, and add the tomatoes and their juice. Sauté for at least another 15 minutes until the liquid from the tomatoes has reduced by half. Add the garlic, red chili flakes, and remaining salt and pepper and cook for 2 to 3 additional minutes.

Add the pasta (boiled to just before al dente) and reserved cup of pasta water. Using tongs, gently lift and fold the pasta into the tomato mixture. Simmer for 2 to 3 minutes, and add roasted veggies and fresh parsley. Transfer to a large serving bowl and top with plenty of grated parmesan and extra virgin olive oil. Garnish with parsley.

Brown Sugar Ribs

PREP TIME: 15 minutes **COOK TIME:** 3 hours **SERVES:** 2 to 4

Brown Sugar Ribs

INGREDIENTS

1 full rack St. Louis–style pork ribs
½ cup Dijon mustard
½ cup brown sugar
1 tablespoon garlic powder
1 tablespoon ground paprika
1 tablespoon onion powder
1 teaspoon ground cayenne pepper
1 teaspoon freshly ground black pepper
1 teaspoon salt

DIRECTIONS

Preheat the oven to 300°. Rub ribs generously on both sides with mustard. Let them stand for at least 15 minutes. In a separate bowl, mix remaining ingredients together to make a rub. Rub the seasonings into the ribs on both sides. Wrap ribs tightly in aluminum foil. Lay the ribs on a foil-lined baking sheet, and bake for 3 hours. Make sure to completely wrap your ribs with the foil. Heat outdoor grill to 350°. Lay ribs on the hot grill, and cook for 30 minutes. Watch for hot spots, and rotate every 7 minutes. These ribs are tasty, tender, and easy, and your family will love them!

PREP TIME: 10 minutes **INACTIVE TIME:** 30 minutes
COOK TIME: Up to 60 minutes **SERVES:** 4 to 6

Caramelized Leek & Bacon Tart

> *This is a brunch must-have!*
> I used a large 10-inch tart pan lined with parchment.

BUTTER PASTRY CRUST

2 cups all-purpose flour
1 cup cold butter, diced
1 teaspoon salt
¼ cup ice water

FILLING

3 cups leeks, cleaned and chopped
1 tablespoon butter
1 tablespoon oil
12 eggs
4 slices of bacon, uncooked and chopped
Pinch of salt
1 teaspoon freshly cracked black pepper
2 cups shredded cheese (I use sharp white cheddar and parmesan)

DIRECTIONS

In the bowl of a food processor, pulse flour, butter, and salt until crumbly. Add water. Pulse 2 to 3 times until it comes together. Pat into a round and wrap in cling film. Chill for at least 30 minutes.

Caramelize leeks in 1 tablespoon butter and 1 tablespoon oil over medium-high heat until they are soft, translucent, and beginning to brown considerably, at least 10 minutes. Set aside and allow to cool.

Prepare Pastry Crust, and allow to chill for at least 30 minutes. If your crust has been chilling longer, allow it to sit on the counter for a few minutes until it's pliable. Roll the crust out on a floured surface until you reach 14 inches all the way around. Gently lay into tart pan or deep-dish pie plate. Trim excess crust, and set aside.

Preheat the oven to 350°. Crack the eggs into a large mixing bowl, and whisk gently to break the yolks and incorporate the eggs. Add chopped bacon, caramelized leeks, salt, pepper, and cheese; mix together thoroughly. Pour into pastry crust. Bake on a baking sheet (to catch any overflow) for 60 minutes. The eggs should puff, and the crust should turn golden brown.

PREP TIME: 5 minutes COOK TIME: 15 to 20 minutes SERVES: 4

Turkey & Chickpea Greek-Style Pitas with Dill Yogurt Sauce

INGREDIENTS

1 pound ground turkey

1 cup canned chickpeas, pulsed in the food processor or coarsely chopped

1 egg

1 teaspoon freshly cracked black pepper

1 teaspoon garlic powder

1 teaspoon kosher salt

1 teaspoon onion powder

Topping suggestions: lettuce, tomato slices, Kalamata olives, sliced onions, sliced cucumbers, hot sauce, crumbled feta cheese, Dill Yogurt Sauce (see recipe below)

DIRECTIONS

Combine all the ingredients except toppings in a mixing bowl, and mix gently with a fork. Form into 8 medium patties, and cook over medium-high heat in an oiled skillet until golden brown on both sides. Serve in soft pita bread, and top with your choice of veggies and sauces.

Dill Yogurt Sauce

1 cup plain Greek yogurt

½ cup chopped fresh dill

2 tablespoons milk

½ teaspoon freshly cracked black pepper

½ teaspoon garlic powder

½ teaspoon kosher salt

½ teaspoon onion powder

DIRECTIONS

Mix and allow melding in the fridge for at least 1 hour before serving. That's it!

PREP TIME: 5 to 10 minutes **COOK TIME:** 5 minutes **SERVES:** 4

Cast-Iron Paprika Shrimp

> Let us be very honest: it took me about 10 to 12 uses out of my preseasoned cast-iron skillet to get a nonstick surface. I was very upset most of the time because I saw so many people using them with ease. Don't feel bad if you're getting a bit of stick on your skillet! Just keep seasoning it, oiling it up, and turning it on to a proper amount of round heat in your oven, and you'll get there!

INGREDIENTS

- 2 pounds 18 to 20 count or larger shrimp, peeled, tail on
- 1 tablespoon olive oil
- 1 to 2 cloves fresh garlic, crushed
- 1 tablespoon ground sweet or hot paprika (if you'd like a kick)
- 2 teaspoons salt
- 1 teaspoon freshly ground black pepper

DIRECTIONS

Heat skillet to medium-high (not high enough to smoke out your house, but a nice, solid, upper side of medium). Shrimp cook lightning-quick. They're cooked once they're opaque and pink the whole way through. Pat shrimp dry with a paper towel, and add to a large mixing bowl. Add the garlic and seasonings, and coat each shrimp evenly. Add the olive oil and butter into the skillet and heat. Lay half the shrimp in the skillet; they will sizzle and look lovely. Turn after about 1 minute. Cook for an additional 1 to 2 minutes on the opposite side. They will be fragrant and pink and look like the letter C; tightly coiled shrimp are overcooked. I do them in two batches so I don't crowd my pan, then I throw them on salad, make a snazzy cocktail, or serve them with a gooey bowl of Creamy Parmesan Soft Polenta (see recipe page 61).

If you do not own a cast-iron skillet, you can pour the oil and seasonings over the shrimp and bake them for 10 to 15 minutes on a cookie sheet in a preheated 425° oven. Delish!

THE MAIN DISH

Classic Chili with Tomatillos & Grass-Fed Beef

PREP TIME: 10 minutes **BRAISE TIME:** 2 hours **SERVES:** 4

Classic Chili with Tomatillos & Grass-Fed Beef

My enamel-coated cast-iron has quickly become my favorite vessel to use during cooler weather. This recipe isn't fussy by any means, and the time in the oven allows everything to marry together brilliantly.

INGREDIENTS

- 1½ pounds grass-fed ground beef (85/15)
- 2 to 3 tablespoons olive oil
- 3 cloves fresh garlic, chopped
- 1 onion, diced
- 1 green bell pepper, diced
- 1 red bell pepper, diced
- 1 tablespoon ground chili powder
- 1 tablespoon ground paprika
- 1 tablespoon ground turmeric
- 3 teaspoons kosher salt
- 2 teaspoons freshly cracked black pepper
- 1 teaspoon garlic powder
- 2 fresh tomatillos, diced
- 1 (16-ounce) can diced tomatoes, with juice
- 3 cups low-sodium beef stock
- 2 (16-ounce) cans red kidney beans, drained

DIRECTIONS

Preheat the oven to 350°. Brown the meat in the olive oil over medium-high heat in an ovenproof pot, preferably enamel-coated cast iron. Remove the meat from the pot, and set aside. Add the garlic, veggies, and spices. Cook in the pan drippings for at least 5 minutes over medium heat. You will notice the spices becoming fragrant. Once the spices are toasted and the veggies are soft, add the tomatillos, the tomatoes and their juice, and the beef stock. Return the meat to the pan, and use a wooden spoon to loosen any brown bits from the bottom. Simmer on the stove for 5 minutes before adding the kidney beans. Place a lid on the pan, and transfer to oven for 2 hours.

Serve with warm Garlic & Cheddar Corn Bread (see recipe page 81)!

PREP TIME: 10 to 15 minutes **COOK TIME:** 5 to 10 minutes **SERVES:** 4

Fettucine in Caper & Parmesan Cream Sauce

INGREDIENTS

½ cup capers, drained

1 shallot, diced

3 tablespoons butter

1 tablespoon olive oil

2 cloves fresh garlic, crushed

Salt and pepper to taste

2 cups heavy cream

½ pound dry pasta, cooked according to package directions

1 cup shredded parmesan cheese

DIRECTIONS

Sauté capers and shallots in butter and oil in a large nonstick sauté pan until they become fragrant and caramelized. This process will take about 5 minutes over medium-high heat. Then add garlic, and cook for only about 1 minute. At this stage, pay close attention so you don't burn the garlic. Add a few turns of cracked black pepper and a pinch of kosher salt.

Pour heavy cream into the pan, and reduce the mixture. Ladle cooked pasta into the cream, and reduce the entire mixture. Once the cream begins to thicken (about 3 minutes), add parmesan cheese and toss. Immediately remove from heat and serve!

PREP TIME: 60 minutes **BAKE TIME:** 60 to 90 minutes **SERVES:** 4

Stuffed Cabbage Rolls

INGREDIENTS

1 head cabbage
1 pound sweet Italian sausage
1 pound ground turkey or beef
6 cloves fresh garlic, chopped, divided
1 (16-ounce) can stewed Italian tomatoes
1½ cups white wine
2 teaspoons kosher salt
1 teaspoon freshly ground black pepper
4 tablespoons short-grain brown rice
1 (16-ounce) can tomato sauce
1 cup chicken stock

DIRECTIONS

Bring cabbage to a simmer with enough water to cover it. Let simmer until tender, at least 20 minutes. Remove and allow to cool for at least 1 hour.

Next, brown the meat and add 3 cloves of garlic, the stewed tomatoes, and wine, along with salt and pepper. Allow this mixture to simmer for about 15 minutes to reduce the liquid. Add brown rice, and turn off the heat. In another saucepan, combine the tomato sauce, remaining garlic, and chicken stock. Bring to a boil, then turn off the heat.

Assembly is great! Preheat the oven to 350°, and butter a 9-by-13-inch baking dish. Remove 1 large leaf of cabbage, fill with 2 to 3 tablespoons of the brown rice/meat mixture, fold into a small package, and place seam side down in a baking dish. Continue this process until all your cabbage is gone. Pour tomato sauce over the finished cabbage rolls, and bake for 2 hours covered with foil. I serve these over buttery mashed potatoes.

PREP TIME: 45 minutes **COOK TIME:** 10 to 15 minutes **SERVES:** 4

Fresh Pasta with White Wine & Butter Sauce

PASTA

2 cups plus 2 tablespoons flour (all-purpose, Semolina or a mix)
3 whole eggs
2 egg yolks
½ teaspoon salt
1 teaspoon olive oil

DIRECTIONS

Make a pile of flour in the center of a dry board or countertop. Using your fist, make an 8-inch well. Crack the eggs, and add them, along with the extra yolks, to the center. Add salt and olive oil. Using a standard table fork, beat the eggs gently in a flat circular motion, incorporating a small amount of flour continuously as you mix. This takes 5 to 7 minutes. Once your dough begins to come together, knead it, and incorporate the final amounts of flour. (You don't need to use every last bit.) Knead with the heels of your hand for at least 7 to 10 minutes. The better you knead the dough, the tastier it will become. Once your pasta has a velvety texture and you can no longer see bits of flour or differing textures, place it inside a plastic container with a flour-dusted lid to rest for at least 30 minutes. (I love a 45-minute rest.) This allows the gluten to relax and the flour to become fully absorbed into the egg. Once rested, roll and cut pasta using a pasta machine. Cook in boiling, salted water 2 to 3 minutes. Meanwhile, prepare White Wine & Butter Sauce. Add cooked pasta to prepared sauce, tossing to coat, and serve.

White Wine & Butter Sauce

1 cup sliced onions
½ cup cold cube butter
2 tablespoons oil

2 cloves fresh garlic, crushed
Salt and pepper to taste
2 cups white wine

Fresh herbs for garnish

DIRECTIONS

Sauté onions in 2 tablespoons butter and 2 tablespoons oil. Once the onions are translucent, turn heat up to medium-high, add garlic and seasonings, and wait for 1 to 2 minutes, stirring continuously. Deglaze pan with wine. Bring to a simmer and reduce by ¼. Add cold butter cube to the pan to thicken; finish with fresh herbs and cracked black pepper. Bathe ravioli, fish, or chicken in this sauce.

PREP TIME: 10 minutes **COOK TIME:** 5 to 7 minutes **SERVES:** 4

Ham & Brie Sandwich

Heaven smiles when this sandwich is made.

I can remember loving ham and Brie, and when we opened Minoela, we wanted a signature sandwich, something that you had to have! It's still my favorite sandwich of all time. Every time I make it, I'm right back in the kitchen at Minoela. For that reason alone, it's pure joy!

INGREDIENTS

- 1 large (24-ounce) French baguette, sliced into 4 sandwich rolls
- ¾ cup Spicy Brown Mustard May Sauce (see recipe below)
- 1 pound thinly sliced Black Forest ham
- 8 ¼-inch slices double cream Brie
- 1 Granny Smith apple, cored and sliced

DIRECTIONS

Preheat oven to 425°, and butterfly sandwich baguettes. Generously smear a few tablespoons of Spicy Brown Mustard Mayo Sauce on both sides of the bread. Add ¼ of the meat to the bread, and lay 2 slices of Brie on top. Bake in a cast-iron skillet or on a cookie sheet for about 7 minutes or until the bread and sauce are golden and bubbly, and the cheese is soft and melted but still holding its shape. Once the sammies are out of the oven, lay at least 4 thin slices of apple on top, and prepare to be wowed!

Spicy Brown Mustard Mayo

- 1 cup good mayonnaise
- ½ cup spicy brown mustard

DIRECTIONS

Mix together. This can stay in the fridge for about two days.

Lemon & Greek Basil Roasted Chicken

PREP TIME: 10 minutes **INACTIVE TIME:** 60 minutes
ROAST TIME: 60 to 90 minutes **SERVES:** 4

Lemon & Greek Basil Roasted Chicken

INGREDIENTS

- 1 4 to 5 pound fresh young whole chicken
- 2 lemons, divided
- 3 tablespoons butter, softened
- 2 tablespoons kosher salt, plus a pinch
- 1 tablespoon freshly cracked black pepper
- 1 teaspoon ground chili powder
- 1 medium sweet onion, sliced
- 4 cloves fresh garlic, crushed, divided
- 1 cup Greek or sweet Italian basil (do not use Thai basil), 2 tablespoons reserved for garnish
- 2 tablespoons olive oil

DIRECTIONS

Rinse fresh chicken and cavity under cold water. Pat the chicken dry with paper towels, and set aside to come to room temperature, at least 1 hour. Preheat the oven to 425°. Slice lemons as thinly as you can while keeping them intact; set aside. Carefully use your hand to separate the skin from the top of the breast meat, but do not remove or tear the skin. Rub the butter inside the breast and all over the outside breast and leg area. Liberally sprinkle seasonings all over the bird, including inside the cavity.

Place half the lemon slices, onion, 2 cloves of garlic, and half the basil in the cavity. Tuck the 2 remaining garlic cloves under the skin of the breast. Place the remaining lemon slices and basil all over the bird but not under the skin. Place the chicken in a roasting pan, pour olive oil all over, and sprinkle with a pinch more kosher salt. Roast in the oven for 30 minutes before reducing the temperature to 375° for 60 to 90 more minutes.

You will get a perfectly cooked, juicy, roasted chicken; I do this entire process uncovered. If the lemon slices begin to get too dark, tent the bird with foil.

PREP TIME: 20 minutes COOK TIME: 3 to 5 minutes SERVES: 4

Farro with Roasted Tomato Vinaigrette & Poached Eggs

FARRO
2 cups cooked farro (in stock, not water)
1 cup grated parmesan cheese
Fresh torn basil to taste

DIRECTIONS
In a large mixing bowl, combine farro, cheese, and fresh basil. Set aside.

Roasted Tomato Vinaigrette
2 cups cherry tomatoes (roasted for 20 minutes at 350° until they begin to burst)
Salt and pepper to taste
½ cup olive oil

Juice of 1 lemon
1 teaspoon Dijon mustard
½ shallot, finely diced
Fresh torn basil to taste

DIRECTIONS
Add the roasted cherry tomatoes, including pan juices, to all other vinaigrette ingredients in another bowl, and mix gently. Pour over the farro mixture. Fold in the dressing gently until all grains are coated.

Poached Egg
Bring a large pot of water to a simmer (do not boil). Make a whirlpool in the center of the water, and crack an egg into the middle. Do not disturb the egg while it's setting. A properly poached egg takes at least 3 minutes. Use a slotted spoon to retrieve the egg from the water, and drain it on a paper towel. Set atop your farro and enjoy!

PREP TIME: 10 minutes **BRAISE TIME:** 3 hours **SERVES:** 4

Perfect Braised Chuck Roast

INGREDIENTS

3 tablespoons butter

4 tablespoons olive oil, divided

3 teaspoons kosher salt

2 teaspoons freshly ground black pepper

2 to 3 pounds chuck roast (nicely marbled with fat)

2 medium onions, sliced

1 bulb fennel, sliced (outer part removed, tops chopped off)

1 cup dry white wine (hard cider is lovely, too)

2 cloves fresh garlic, chopped

2 cups unsalted beef stock

1 sprig fresh rosemary

DIRECTIONS

Preheat the oven to 350°. Melt butter and 3 tablespoons olive oil together in an enamel-coated cast-iron Dutch oven. Rub salt and pepper all over the meat, and sear or brown roast on all sides, about 3 minutes a side. Once roast is browned, set it aside on a plate. Add onions and fennel to the pot with additional 1 tablespoon oil. Add wine to deglaze the pan, and use a wooden spoon to scrape the bottom of the pan to loosen browned bits. Add chopped garlic, beef stock, and rosemary; return beef to the pot; and cook covered for 3 hours. Check halfway through on the liquid; the idea is to have enough to come up the sides of the meat. Add a bit more stock if needed. Turn the oven off after 3 hours, and let the roast sit for 30 minutes. Allow an additional 10 to 15 minutes of resting time outside the oven. Serve with mashed potatoes and butter or Creamy Parmesan Soft Polenta (see recipe page 61).

Spicy Kalamata Puttanesca

PREP TIME: 10 minutes **COOK TIME:** 90 to 120 minutes **SERVES:** 4

Spicy Kalamata Puttanesca

INGREDIENTS

5 to 6 medium anchovy fillets
¼ cup olive oil
1 teaspoon red pepper flakes
1 teaspoon salt
1 teaspoon freshly ground black pepper
1 large yellow or Spanish onion, diced
7 cloves fresh garlic, minced
½ cup butter
1 cup pitted Kalamata olives
1 cup black oil-cured olives
2 cups white wine
2 (28-ounce) cans San Marzano or whole peeled tomatoes
1 cup diced fresh tomatoes
½ pound dry linguine or spaghetti, cooked according to package directions

DIRECTIONS

Brown anchovies in the oil in a large soup pot or enamel-covered cast-iron Dutch oven over medium heat until the anchovies smell nutty-buttery and all the fillets have dissolved completely into the oil. Add the red pepper flakes, salt, and pepper, and continue to cook for about 3 minutes to toast the seasonings. Add the onion, and cook about 10 minutes until the onion becomes tender. Add the garlic, and sauté for 2 to 3 minutes. Do not brown the garlic. Add the butter and olives, and cook for another 10 minutes. Add the wine, increase heat to medium-high, and simmer for 5 minutes. Add all the tomatoes, and simmer on low for at least 1 to 1½ hours. After 2 hours, the sauce will be thick and rich and will taste lovely paired with any pasta or Creamy Parmesan Soft Polenta (see recipe page 61).

PREP TIME: 10 to 15 minutes **BRAISE TIME:** 3 hours **SERVES:** 4

Wine-Drenched Beef Short Ribs

INGREDIENTS

1 cup flour

4 teaspoons kosher salt, divided

2 teaspoons freshly ground black pepper, divided

3 pounds meaty, thick-cut beef short ribs

3 tablespoons butter

2 tablespoons olive oil

1 medium yellow onion, sliced and halved

2 leeks, cleaned and sliced into quarters

4 cloves fresh garlic, chopped

1 (750-milliliter) bottle pinot noir or French blend (you want a light, juicy red)

1 sprig fresh thyme

1 sprig fresh rosemary

2 cups unsalted beef stock

Fresh, diced flat-leaf parsley to finish

DIRECTIONS

Preheat the oven to 350°. Mix flour, 1 teaspoon salt, and 1 teaspoon pepper in a brown paper bag. Add the meat, and shake the bag to coat evenly. Dust the excess flour off the meat. Melt the butter and olive oil in a large, enamel-coated Dutch oven over medium-high heat. Add the ribs, and brown on all sides, about 10 minutes. (Do not overcrowd the pan, or you will have gray meat; you're looking for golden brown, but not cooked. It's fine to brown meat in 2 separate batches.) Remove meat from the pan, and add onion and leeks. Cook for about 5 minutes over medium heat. Then add garlic, and cook for 1 additional minute. Deglaze pan with the entire bottle of wine. Add meat back, and make sure to loosen the brown bits off the bottom with a wooden spoon. Add herbs, beef stock, and remaining salt and pepper. Place the entire pot in the oven for 3 hours. It feels like a long time, but it's the perfect amount to make the meat extra-tender, and the entire flavor will meld!

Don't forget to use the fresh parsley to garnish your wonderful dinner!

THE MAIN DISH 143

Quick Cashew Chicken

PREP TIME: 10 minutes **COOK TIME:** 10 minutes **SERVES:** 4

Quick Cashew Chicken

Sometimes you need dinner on the table to feed your family in 20 minutes or less. By the time the white rice is cooked, you will have a tasty Chinese-inspired American dish that's guilt-free and reminds me of takeout.

SLURRY

3 teaspoons cornstarch
¼ cup water or chicken stock
1 tablespoon rice vinegar

CASHEW CHICKEN

1 pound boneless, skinless chicken breast, cut into 1-inch cubes
2 tablespoons light-tasting oil
2½ teaspoons salt, divided
2 teaspoons freshly ground black pepper, divided
¼ teaspoon red chili flakes
1 medium onion, thinly sliced
2 to 3 baby bok choy, sliced
2 to 3 dinosaur kale leaves, sliced
3 to 4 broccoli florets, thinly sliced
6 cloves garlic, minced
3 cups chicken stock
3 tablespoons hoisin sauce
4 cups cooked white rice
1 cup toasted cashews for garnish
1 cup chopped green onions for garnish
Hot sauce, optional

DIRECTIONS

First, make cornstarch slurry by combining cornstarch, water or stock, and vinegar, and set aside.

Then, in a wok or large deep skillet, sauté chicken in oil over medium-high heat. Add 1 teaspoon of salt, 1 teaspoon of pepper, and red chili flakes. After 2 to 3 minutes, add onions, and sauté until they begin to soften. Add the veggies and garlic, along with the remaining salt and pepper. Add chicken stock; it will quickly come to a simmer. Add hoisin sauce, and mix thoroughly. Add cornstarch slurry, careful to stir quickly so it doesn't seize. It will thicken slightly, and you will have a glossy, beautiful dish. Spoon over rice, and top with plenty of toasted cashews, green onions, and hot sauce, if you like!

Baked Copper River Salmon with Spicy Pineapple Salsa

PREP TIME: 5 to 10 minutes **BAKE TIME:** 10 to 15 minutes **SERVES:** 4

Baked Copper River Salmon with Spicy Pineapple Salsa

I am simple with protein, and baking the perfect medium salmon is one of my all-time favorite ways to prepare it. Copper River salmon is the king of all salmon, and its fatty, rich texture is perfect for Spicy Sweet Pineapple Salsa. When we make this, I make enough for lunch the next day and maybe a snack after dinner!

INGREDIENTS

2 pounds fresh salmon fillets, cut into 4 8-ounce portions
Salt and pepper to taste
Olive oil
Spicy Sweet Pineapple Salsa (see recipe below)

DIRECTIONS

Preheat the oven to 425°. Lay the salmon on a glass baking dish, and sprinkle with salt and pepper. Drizzle with olive oil. Bake for 10 to 15 minutes or until salmon is opaque and cooked through. Remove from the oven, and let set for 3 to 5 minutes in the pan to continue cooking. Your salmon will be medium and slightly underdone in the center. If you like a well-done piece of fish, bake for an additional few minutes. Top each portion with at least ½ cup of Spicy Sweet Pineapple Salsa. This recipe can easily be substituted for ANY type of salmon.

Spicy Sweet Pineapple Salsa

2 cups fresh pineapple, diced into small cubes
½ sweet onion, diced
½ cup chopped fresh cilantro
1 medium sweet red bell pepper, diced
Salt and pepper to taste
Juice and zest of 1 lime
1 teaspoon red chili flakes

DIRECTIONS

This stuff is addictive and guilt-free. The salty-spicy-sweet combo is a match made in chicken or fish heaven. Simply mix all the ingredients, and allow to sit at room temperature for at least 1 hour before serving.

PREP TIME: 10 minutes **SERVES:** 4

Thai Rice Salad

INGREDIENTS

2 cups wild or brown rice, cooked
1 cucumber, diced
1 red bell pepper, diced
½ cup chopped cilantro
½ cup olive oil
½ cup salted dry roasted peanuts
½ cup shredded carrots
Juice of 1 lime (2 if the yield isn't juicy)
2 tablespoons rice vinegar
1 tablespoon honey
1 tablespoon sesame seeds
1 tablespoon Thai chili paste
1 clove fresh garlic, crushed
¼ teaspoon sesame oil

DIRECTIONS

I love simple recipes, and for this one, you simply add everything to a bowl and mix! Allow to sit for at least 1 hour before serving. Add any grilled meat to make it a main dish.

PREP TIME: 15 minutes **COOK TIME:** 10 to 15 minutes **SERVES:** 4

Strozzapreti in Gorgonzola & Pancetta Cream Sauce

INGREDIENTS

5 slices of pancetta or center-cut bacon, diced

1 cup onion, diced or sliced

1 red pepper, thinly sliced

1 tablespoon butter

2 cloves garlic, smashed

3 cups heavy cream

Salt and pepper to taste

½ pound dry strozzapreti pasta (or any short pasta), cooked according to package directions

1 cup pasta-cooking liquid, reserved

1 cup parmesan cheese

½ cup crumbled Gorgonzola

DIRECTIONS

Cook the bacon, onion, and red pepper in the butter in a nonstick skillet over medium heat until the bacon begins to caramelize and the onions are soft. Add the garlic, and cook for another minute or so, being careful not to burn. This process takes up to 15 minutes. Add the cream, and season with salt and pepper. Reduce the cream by ¼. Using a wooden spoon, loosen the brown bits (or fond) from the bottom of the pan. This is all excellent flavor that adds richness to your sauce base. The sauce will begin to bubble and thicken. Add cooked pasta and the reserved cooking liquid. Do not add water. (You may use chicken stock if you wish to skip the cooking liquid.) Add cheeses, and stir just to combine. This pasta will be gooey and very flavorful.

PREP TIME: 15 minutes **COOK TIME:** 45 to 60 minutes
YIELDS: one 9×13-inch pan

Creamy, Spicy Tomato Lasagna

INGREDIENTS

6 cups whole milk

½ cup butter, softened

2 tablespoons olive oil

3 cloves fresh garlic, minced

1 teaspoon sea salt

1 teaspoon freshly ground black pepper

¼ cup all-purpose flour

1 (4-ounce) can tomato paste

3 cups parmesan cheese, divided

3 cups mozzarella, divided

1 box no-boil lasagna noodles

3 cups fresh spinach leaves, divided

1 cup halved cherry tomatoes, divided

DIRECTIONS

Heat the milk in a medium saucepan over medium heat. Do not boil or scald; heat only until the milk is almost too hot to touch. Set aside. Melt butter with olive oil in another saucepan over medium heat. Add the garlic salt, pepper, and red pepper flakes, and cook until fragrant, 2 to 3 minutes. Sprinkle in the flour, and stir to create a roux. Cook for another 2 to 3 minutes, until roux is thick, blond, and creamy. Slowly add the heated milk. Cook until the sauce begins to thicken, about 10 minutes, stirring constantly with a wire whisk. Add the tomato paste, and fully incorporate until you have a rich sauce. Remove from the heat, and add 1 cup parmesan and ½ cup mozzarella. Stir to combine.

Preheat the oven to 350°, and oil a 9×13-inch lasagna pan. Ladle 1 cup of the sauce on the bottom of the pan. Layer ⅛ of the noodles over the sauce, and cover with ⅛ of the remaining sauce. Top with ½ the spinach, ⅛ of the remaining cheeses, and ½ the cherry tomatoes. Repeat this process (noodles, sauce, spinach, cheese, and tomatoes) once, then top with remaining noodles, remaining sauce, and remaining cheeses. Cover with foil, and bake on a cookie sheet for 45 to 60 minutes. For the last 15 minutes, remove foil so the cheese can brown and bubble on top.

Remove lasagna from the oven, and let stand for 15 minutes before slicing! I like to serve this with a little spoonful of fresh marinara over the top and an extra sprinkle of cheese.

PREP TIME: 10 minutes **COOK TIME:** 15 minutes **SERVES:** 4

Chicken Sausage & Tortellini Pasta Salad

INGREDIENTS

1 (8-ounce) package dry mini tortellini or ravioli, cooked according to package instructions

1 pound chicken sausage links, browned and sliced into coins

3 cups baby spinach

1½ cups diced fresh tomato

1 cup shredded parmesan cheese

1 cup pitted olives

1 cup bottled Italian dressing

¼ cup olive oil

Juice of 1 lemon

½ cup chopped fresh basil

Salt and pepper to taste

DIRECTIONS

Add the cooked pasta and sausage to a large mixing bow. Add the rest of the ingredients in order of appearance. Mix and chill, or enjoy immediately.

PREP TIME: 10 to 15 minutes **BRAISE TIME:** 4 hours **SERVES:** 4

Spanish-Style Braised Chicken

Although this dish is Spanish-inspired, my favorite olives hale from Italy. The mighty Castelvetrano is mild, buttery, and meaty.

INGREDIENTS

2 tablespoons olive oil
1 Spanish onion, sliced
1 whole chicken, quartered
4 cups unsalted chicken stock
2 cups pitted green olives (I used Castelvetrano)
1 (6-ounce) can tomato paste
2 cloves fresh garlic, crushed
1 tablespoon freshly ground black pepper
1 tablespoon ground paprika
1 tablespoon ground turmeric
1 tablespoon onion powder
1 tablespoon salt

DIRECTIONS

Preheat the oven to 300°. Coat the bottom of an enamel-covered Dutch oven or ovenproof stewing pot with oil. Lay in the onion slices. Everything else can go right in the pot! Braise for 3 hours. Using a ladle, move the seasonings about in the liquid to make sure everything is well-incorporated. Remove the lid, and increase the heat to 350° for the last hour. Serve over jasmine rice or with warm pita bread for sopping up the rich broth.

FROM LEFT: Picnic Dog, Cuban Dog, Southern Italian Dog, Hot Seattle Dog, Kraut Master, Chicago Dog

The Kraut Master amd The Chicago Dog

Hot Dogs

> These hot dogs were among my very first real styling jobs. We were tasked by our client to come up with several fun and inspired recipes, and I was thrilled. I made sure to give Noah his very own hot dog as we set up the photo shoot. I felt so proud watching Mike make the photos in our living room, which was completely transformed into a set. It was messy and frustrating and so much fun. Seeing our hard work in the form of the greatest hot dog spread was so rewarding. It'll forever be a pretty special thing for us, those hot dogs, that apartment, and those tiny baby hands clutching hot dogs as we worked. It felt like the promise of a brand-new beginning. Who knew all of that could be summed up in one great bite?

Cuban Dog
Wagyu hot dog, thin Black Forest ham, baby Swiss, whole-grain mustard, kosher dill pickle spear

Picnic Dog
Wagyu dog, bourbon-baked beans, kettle-cooked potato chips

Southern Italian Dog
Wagyu dog, baby arugula, sun-dried tomato aioli, whole sweet roasted garlic

Kraut Master
¾ pound bratwurst, Quick Homemade Sauerkraut (see recipe page 256), German whole-grain mustard

Hot Seattle Dog or Drunk Dog
Wagyu dog, jalapeños, pepperoncinis, sweet cherry peppers, cream cheese

Chicago Dog
¾ pound bratwurst, traditional slaw, pickle spears, tomato slices

To Drink

*Take out a tall glass.
Let's refresh!*

Let's step away from the table for a moment and move to the cupboard. Take out a tall glass. Let's refresh!

Sometimes a beverage as simple as water with fresh berries or mint is the best renewal. Nothing washes away worries like a warm cup of tea or hot cocoa. Let's not kid ourselves: a shot of tequila with muddled lime, sipped on ice, has a tendency to refresh like a scripture or a good night's sleep. When a special drink is shared with a friend, or perhaps enjoyed quietly while alone with your thoughts after a busy week, it can be just what you need to keep going.

Enjoy the beautiful cocktails and lovely flavored-water suggestions.

PREP TIME: 20 minutes **YIELDS:** one large pitcher

Blackberry Mint Water

[Flavored waters are my favorite way to make any summertime gathering a bit more elegant.

INGREDIENTS
Large pitcher filled halfway with ice
Water
1 cup fresh mint, any varietal (pineapple mint is lovely)
1 cup fresh blackberries

DIRECTIONS
Simply place your desired flavoring on ice, and fill the pitcher with water. Let it steep for at least 20 minutes before serving. By the way, you might find brown spots on the mint after steeping. If so, add fresh mint before serving.

Other great combinations are white grapes and strawberries or cucumbers and melons. Use a sharp veggie peeler to shave cantaloupe and cucumber with the rind on; it makes for a beautiful presentation.

PREP TIME: 5 minutes **SERVES:** 2

Blood Orange Whiskey Cocktail

One evening, while my son and husband were on an outing, I thought, *Time to bust out the girly magazines, turn on reality TV, and enjoy a little Mommy alone time.* There was just something missing, though: a cocktail and a salty snack! While I snacked on a few cashews, I looked through our liquor cabinet, hoping to find a little tequila, but I was disappointed to see only a bottle of aged whiskey. Hmm…whiskey wasn't what came to mind during my relaxing thoughts, but then again, why not see whether I couldn't turn this into something tasty? I was right. Let's just say that old bottle of whiskey didn't last much longer after my husband returned and we found out it was so darn tasty in a cocktail.

INGREDIENTS

15 raspberries
¼ cup fresh lime juice
1 cup freshly squeezed blood orange juice
2 ounces whiskey
Ice

DIRECTIONS

Add the raspberries and lime juice to a cocktail shaker, and muddle. Add the juice and whiskey. Fill the shaker with ice, and get to shaking! I love an icy cocktail with chips floating about. Pour into a chilled glass, and enjoy. This recipe makes two large cocktails.

Chilly Hot Chocolate

PREP TIME: 5 minutes **SERVES:** 2

Chilly Hot Chocolate

INGREDIENTS

½ cup cream

¼ teaspoon salt

Zest of 1 orange

1 habanero pepper

½ cup dark chocolate pieces

1 ounce Grand Marnier or any orange liqueur

3 scoops Mukilteo Mudd Ice Cream (from Snoqualmie Ice Cream)

Fresh Whipped Cream (see recipe page 251) and candied orange zest, optional

DIRECTIONS

Add cream, salt, orange zest, and pepper to a small saucepan, and simmer over medium heat for 5 to 10 minutes. The longer you steep your cream, the spicier it will become. Depending on how hot you want your shake, you could split the end of the pepper before adding it; this allows the heat to perfume the cream thoroughly. If you like less of a kick, don't cut your pepper. After 10 minutes, discard the pepper, and allow cream to cool. I prefer to chill it.

In a blender, combine the cool cream and the rest of the ingredients. Blend until you've got a thick, creamy shake. Pour into chilled glasses, and top with Fresh Whipped Cream or candied orange zest!

PREP TIME: 5 minutes **SERVES:** 1

Crème Fraîche Strawberry Bourbon Shake

This cool treat is the perfect mix between a sundae and a boozy shake!

INGREDIENTS

½ cup strawberries

2 tablespoons sugar

3 scoops crème fraîche gelato (I used Snoqualmie Ice Cream)

¼ cup cream

¼ teaspoon salt

¼ cup Salted Toffee Sauce (see recipe page 251), divided

1 ounce bourbon

¼ cup crushed pretzels, divided

Fresh Whipped Cream (see recipe page 251), optional

DIRECTIONS

Blend the strawberries and sugar to make a puree; set aside. Blend the gelato, cream, and salt; set aside. Pour the strawberry puree into the bottom of a glass, add bourbon, and add half the toffee sauce. Sprinkle half the crushed pretzels over the toffee. Scoop the gelato mixture on top, drizzle with remaining toffee sauce, and sprinkle on remaining pretzels! Fresh Whipped Cream is a nice touch as well.

Creamy Bourbon Float

PREP TIME: 5 minutes **SERVES:** 4

Creamy Bourbon Float

> *I like bourbon. I like ice cream.*
> Bourbon has a sweet, smoky caramel undertone that gets me. When you mix bourbon and creamy vanilla ice cream with cream soda, something magical happens: you're a grown-up kid with a warm and chilly drink perfect for a cozy evening.

INGREDIENTS

4 ounces bourbon
4 large scoops vanilla ice cream
4 bottles cream soda
Fresh Whipped Cream (see recipe page 251)
Caramel to drizzle

DIRECTIONS

Add 1 ounce of bourbon to each of 4 glasses. Add 1 scoop of ice cream, then top with cream soda. Top with Fresh Whipped Cream and drizzled caramel for an even better treat!

PREP TIME: 5 minutes **SERVES:** 1

Espresso Ice Cream Float

[*Floats aren't just for sodas anymore!*

INGREDIENTS

1 ounce Kahlua or coffee liqueur
3 scoops Snoqualmie Espresso ice cream
½ cup cream
2 cold shots of espresso

DIRECTIONS

Pour the liqueur into the bottom of a glass, and add ice cream. Add cream and then espresso over the top!

PREP TIME: 15 minutes **SERVES:** 8

Fresh Minted Limeade

INGREDIENTS

Juice of 10 to 12 medium limes

1½ cups sugar, divided

1 cup fresh mint leaves

6 to 8 cups water

¼ cup superfine sugar (to rim glasses)

1 cup fresh blueberries

Sprigs of fresh mint for garnish

DIRECTIONS

Squeeze limes into a pitcher. If your limes are not very juicy, throw them in the microwave for 10 seconds to bring back a little life.

Slowly add the first cup of sugar. Taste the syrup: if your limes are a bit sweet, you will not need the rest of the sugar. If your syrup tastes too tart, add the rest of the sugar, and continue to taste. This is a personal recipe! Once syrup is to your liking, add fresh mint leaves. Muddle or bruise the leaves with a stirring spoon. After the leaves have a bit of bruising, add the water! Start with the first 6 cups. If limeade tastes too strong, add a touch more water, but this should be perfect!

Pour the superfine sugar on a flat plate. Prepare another flat plate with a few tablespoons of water. Dip the rims of your glasses in the water, then roll the rims in the sugar. I prefer my juice on the tart side, so a sweet rim is refreshing! Sprinkle blueberries on top of each drink, and garnish with a sprig of fresh mint.

Cherry Ginger Beer Margarita (Ginger Beerita)

PREP TIME: 5 minutes **SERVES:** 2

Cherry Ginger Beer Margarita (Ginger Beerita)

INGREDIENTS

½ cup cherry or pomegranate juice

2 ounces tequila

1 ounce triple sec

Juice and zest of 1 lime

1 teaspoon sugar

Ice

Salt for the rim

1 cup ginger beer (use your favorite)

DIRECTIONS

In a cocktail shaker, combine all the ingredients except the salt and ginger beer, and shake vigorously. Evenly pour contents into 2 glasses that have been filled with ice and rimmed with salt. Top each with ½ cup ginger beer.

Old-Fashioned Drinking Chocolate

PREP TIME: 10 minutes **SERVES:** 5

Old-Fashioned Drinking Chocolate

INGREDIENTS

1 cup bittersweet chocolate chips
¼ cup unsweetened cocoa powder
¾ cup granulated sugar
½ teaspoon salt
4 to 5 cups whole milk
1 teaspoon vanilla extract
Chocolate shavings and marshmallow cream, to top

DIRECTIONS

Melt the chocolate chips slowly over low to medium heat. Add the cocoa powder, granulated sugar, and salt. Slowly add the milk, and stir continuously. Bring to a simmer, but do not boil. Remove from the heat, and add vanilla. Pour into mugs, and top with marshmallow cream and chocolate shavings!

PREP TIME: 10 minutes **SERVES:** 5

White Sangria

INGREDIENTS

4 cups white wine (use your favorite)
5 cups brut champagne
½ cup Lemon Simple Syrup (see recipe page 249)
2 cups raspberries
2 white peaches, sliced
1 cup Rainier cherries, pitted

DIRECTIONS

Gently pour wine, champagne, and simple syrup into the bottom of a large pitcher. Gently drop in the fruit, and use a spoon to lightly swirl your tasty mixture! Allow to steep in the refrigerator for at least 1 hour. Pour into tall glasses, and enjoy!

PREP TIME: 10 minutes **SERVES:** 4

Ginger Lemon Soda

> I happen to really enjoy soda, but I don't drink much these days. I will still drink it every once in a while, but if I want to enjoy a bubbly crisp soda with a touch of lemony heat on a warm summery day, this soda comes to mind.

INGREDIENTS

1 cup sugar

½ cup water

½ cup lemon juice

1-inch piece fresh ginger, sliced

1 (24-ounce) bottle sparkling water

DIRECTIONS

Bring sugar, water, lemon juice, and ginger to a simmer over medium heat until the sugar dissolves and the syrup has come together, about 10 minutes. Remove from the heat, and cool completely. You can store this syrup in an airtight container for up to 3 weeks. The ginger will become spicier as it steeps, so it's up to you whether to remove it or keep it in the syrup. To complete the soda, pour 2 ounces of the syrup in the bottom of a tall chilled glass. Top with a few ice cubes, and fill the glass with 4 to 6 ounces of sparkling water!

Sweets

Sweets have this magic ability to part the curtains and let in the light.

We had no freezer at Minoela. When I was dreaming up ideas for sweets to serve, I wanted something cold and creamy that wasn't whipped cream, something special that could accompany the chocolate cake and pound cakes our customers loved. Brown sugar cream was the answer.

As a teenager, I'd visit my friend's house after school, and her grandmother would give us a bowl of strawberries alongside a small dish of sour cream and another filled with real brown sugar. You were supposed to dip the berry in the sour cream, then dunk it in the brown sugar. My mind was blown. I had no idea this was possible. What an invention!

So years later, I thought I might gently swirl the two together and add vanilla and salt. Brown sugar cream was born. This tangy yet bright sweet cream topped *everything* at Minoela. It was so complex yet simple. To this day, I've never tired of it. Our signature dessert became this moist homemade pound cake topped with brown sugar cream and any fresh berries. It'd change to stewed apples or pears in the fall and winter and go right back to sweet, ripe berries in the spring and summer.

There was a quartet of friends who would come in each week to enjoy the cake and cream. They'd visit and talk and laugh. They'd leave their fluffy dog outside, and we'd put out a bowl of water for him. At one point, I noticed one of the friends, visit after visit, had begun walking slower, his eyes tired. He appeared frail. But they continued coming in, ordering the cake, and enjoying themselves, sometimes bringing other friends of theirs and ordering round after round of coffee.

One week, the four friends came in, the frail one being pushed in a wheelchair. Cake, as usual. They sat quietly and sipped coffee. Week after week, they came, these four friends.

And then, one day, there were only three of them. The man I'd watched grow frailer with each passing week was absent.

The three friends ordered cake and lit a birthday candle, sharing fond memories of their departed friend. They sang and laughed and cried, and when they left, I cried, too. I felt so honored to have somehow taken part in that man's story, honored that a cake I made contributed in some small way to the routine of his life and aided his friends in their grieving. This cake with the brown sugar cream truly brings joy. It's one of the best things I've ever made.

Sweets have this magic ability to part the curtains and let in the light. Sugar is a vehicle for delight. A meal isn't truly, properly over without dessert at the end—it's what the rest of the meal leads up to. It's the grand finale, the swan song. Every delectable treat in the following pages will make your day better. Count on it.

PREP TIME: 15 minutes **COOK TIME:** 12 minutes
INACTIVE TIME: 30 to 45 minutes

Butter Toffee

INGREDIENTS

2 cups crushed, salted, roasted nuts, divided

1½ cups butter

1 cup packed dark brown sugar

1 cup unpacked brown sugar

2 cups milk chocolate pieces

DIRECTIONS

Butter a cookie sheet. Place a cookie cooling rack underneath. Sprinkle 1 cup of nuts in the center of the sheet, forming a rectangle at least 7×10 to 8×12 inches in size.

Melt butter and brown sugars in a heavy-bottomed saucepan over medium heat for about 12 minutes. Bring it to a soft boil, not stirring, so that it reaches 285° on a candy dial. Pour quickly over nuts, and sprinkle with chocolate. Let the heat of the candy melt the chocolate, then spread it evenly. Sprinkle remaining 1 cup of nuts over the chocolate. Place in fridge for 30 minutes or until set. Break or cut with a knife. Rustic is best.

PREP TIME: 5 minutes **BAKE TIME:** 60 minutes
INACTIVE TIME: 2 hours **YIELDS:** 4

Almond Pavlova

INGREDIENTS

3 extra-large egg whites, room temperature
½ cup granulated sugar
¼ teaspoon kosher salt
1 teaspoon cornstarch
½ cup almond flour
1 teaspoon vanilla extract

DIRECTIONS

Preheat the oven to 200°. Whip the egg whites and sugar for about 2 minutes on high, until firm, glossy peaks form. Gently fold in the cornstarch, almond flour, and vanilla. Divide batter into 4 equal parts, and drop evenly onto a parchment-lined baking sheet. Bake for 60 minutes. Turn the oven off, and allow the pavlovas to cool inside the oven for 2 hours. Serve by topping with Fresh Whipped Cream (see recipe page 251), berries, and syrup (below).

YIELDS: 2 to 3 cups

Strawberry Syrup

[I normally make this in advance, and it will keep beautifully in the fridge for up to 1 week or in the freezer for up to 3 months.

INGREDIENTS

5 cups fresh strawberries
3 cups sugar (I use evaporated cane juice, but any sugar will do)
2 tablespoons lemon juice

DIRECTIONS

Hull and slice 5 cups of freshly washed strawberries, and add them to a large, nonreactive saucepan with the sugar. Bring the mix to a boil that cannot be stirred down; this process takes about 10 solid minutes. Once the syrup is cooked, remove from the heat and add lemon juice. Place a metal sieve over a clean bowl, and pour the hot berries into the sieve. Mix and smash the berries to drain the syrup into the bowl.

PREP TIME: 5 minutes **BAKE TIME:** 18 to 22 minutes
YIELDS: one 9×13-inch pan

Almond Butter Brownies

INGREDIENTS

2 cups sugar

1 cup almond butter

½ cup butter, softened

4 eggs

1 teaspoon salt

1 cup dark chocolate chips, melted and slightly cooled

¾ cup all-purpose flour

½ cup dark cocoa powder

½ teaspoon baking soda

Flaky sea salt, optional

DIRECTIONS

Preheat the oven to 350°, and line a 9×13-inch pan with parchment.

Mix the first 5 ingredients until they are creamy and smooth; gently fold in the rest. Do not overmix. Pour the batter into the pan, and bake for 18 to 22 minutes. You want these brownies to feel slightly underdone. They are AMAZING!

Banana Bread Made with Greek Yogurt & Pepitas

PREP TIME: 5 minutes **BAKE TIME:** 25 to 35 minutes
YIELDS: one standard loaf pan

Banana Bread Made with Greek Yogurt & Pepitas

INGREDIENTS

3 very ripe bananas, mashed
1 cup dark brown sugar
¾ cup Greek yogurt
¼ cup butter, softened
2 eggs
2 tablespoons coconut oil
1 tablespoon baking powder
1 tablespoon vanilla extract
1 teaspoon ground cinnamon
1 teaspoon salt
1½ cups all-purpose flour
½ cup crushed walnuts
¼ cup pepitas, toasted (optional)

DIRECTIONS

Preheat the oven to 350°, and butter loaf pan. Combine all the ingredients except flour, walnuts, and pepitas, and mix until it's just come together. (I use a light hand mixing baked goods, or else I am prone to creating hockey pucks!) Gently fold in flour and walnuts until it's just mixed. Pour into the buttered loaf pan, and sprinkle with toasted pepitas. Bake for 25 minutes or until a toothpick comes out clean but not squeaky clean.

Enjoy with melty, soft butter!

PREP TIME: 5 minutes **INACTIVE TIME:** 30 minutes
BAKE TIME: 45 minutes **YIELDS:** one 9×13-inch pan

Apple Cranberry Crisp with Vanilla Pouring Cream

FILLING

1 cup dried cranberries
½ cup apple juice
2 tablespoons lemon juice
4 to 5 large tart apples (peel them if the skin is tough)
¾ cup brown sugar
¼ cup melted butter
2 tablespoons all-purpose flour
1 teaspoon salt

OAT CRUMBLE TOPPING

2 cups oats
¾ cup brown sugar
½ cup all-purpose flour
½ cup melted butter
1 tablespoon ground cinnamon
1 teaspoon baking powder
½ teaspoon salt

DIRECTIONS

Preheat the oven to 350°, and liberally butter a 9×13-inch baking dish. Soak the cranberries in the apple and lemon juices for at least 30 minutes. Thinly slice the apples, and lay them in the buttered pan. Evenly sprinkle the remaining filling ingredients over the apples, starting with the soaked cranberries and including half the soaking liquid. Gently mix it all together with a fork.

In a separate bowl, combine all the topping ingredients. Evenly sprinkle over the apple mixture. Bake for at least 45 minutes, until bubbly and golden. (You're looking for thick bubbles while it's still in the oven.) Allow to cool for at least 15 minutes before serving. This is awesome for breakfast, too! Top with Vanilla Pouring Cream (recipe below).

Vanilla Pouring Cream

1 cup heavy cream
2 tablespoons confectioners' sugar
1 teaspoon vanilla extract
¼ teaspoon salt

DIRECTIONS

Vanilla Pouring Cream is simply genius. Mix the cream until it starts to thicken slightly (you don't want whipped cream, but you do want it to thicken up a bit); add sugar, vanilla, and salt; and continue to mix until the sugar is dissolved. Pour over warm crisp.

PREP TIME: 10 to 15 minutes **BAKE TIME:** 12 minutes
YIELDS: 2 dozen cookies

Perfect Apricot & Chocolate Chunk Oatmeal Cookies

> The best cookies are easy drop cookies: warm and gooey with the right amount of chew. Stand mixers are wonderful, but I like a good ol' hand mixer for these cookies!

INGREDIENTS

- 1 cup room-temperature butter, softened
- 2 cups unpacked dark brown sugar
- 1 teaspoon salt
- 1 teaspoon vanilla extract
- 2 eggs
- 2¼ cups oats
- 1 shy cup flour
- 1 cup dark chocolate pieces
- ¾ cup dried apricots, diced
- ¾ cup pecans or hazelnuts, chopped and toasted

DIRECTIONS

Preheat oven to 350°. Mix butter, sugar, salt, and vanilla, then add the eggs one at a time, mixing slightly after each addition. Add the oats, flour, chocolate, fruit, and nuts. Mix until just combined, and drop 6 to 8 spoonfuls of dough onto a parchment-lined cookie sheet. Repeat until dough is used up. Bake for 12 minutes. The cookie might still be a touch glossy in the center, with golden edges. Bake for 1 additional minute if they need a bit more browning. Allow to cool for at least 5 to 7 minutes on the cookie sheet before placing them to cool on wire racks.

INACTIVE TIME: 3 hours **BAKE TIME:** 1 hour **YIELDS:** one 9×13-inch pan

Bread Pudding

> I have a different way of making bread pudding. It is simple and, literally, foolproof!

INGREDIENTS

6 to 7 cups torn, stale Italian country bread (crumbs and all)

3 cups whole milk

2 cups heavy cream

5 eggs

2 teaspoons salt

1 tablespoon vanilla extract

2 cups loosely packed dark brown sugar

1 teaspoon ground cinnamon

½ cup butter, softened, divided

2 cups diced Italian plums (optional)

Salted Toffee Sauce (see recipe page 251)

DIRECTIONS

Soak the bread in the milk and cream (at room temperature) for at least 1 hour; 2 is best. Whip the eggs, salt, vanilla, sugar, and cinnamon until the eggs have given up all elasticity. Fold the eggs into the bread mixture, along with the plums, and mix well. Soak in the refrigerator for at least 2 additional hours and up to overnight! Preheat the oven to 350°, and liberally butter a 9×13-inch baking dish with at least 2 tablespoons of butter. Pour the bread pudding into the dish. Use the remaining butter to dot the top. Bake for at least 1 hour. The pudding will puff up and soufflé. Drizzle with fresh Salted Toffee Sauce and cream or additional butter. Serve warm!

Buttermilk Vanilla Pound Cake

PREP TIME: 5 minutes **BAKE TIME:** 45 to 55 minutes
YIELDS: one Bundt pan

Buttermilk Vanilla Pound Cake

INGREDIENTS

1 cup buttermilk
¾ cup olive oil
½ cup melted butter
5 eggs
2 teaspoons vanilla extract
1½ cups sugar or evaporated cane juice
2¼ cups all-purpose flour
2 tablespoons baking powder
¾ teaspoon sea salt

DIRECTIONS

Preheat oven to 350°, and butter and flour a Bundt or loaf pan. Mix all the wet ingredients until combined. Slowly add the sugar, flour, baking powder, and salt, and mix just until the mixture comes together; don't overmix. Bake for 45 to 55 minutes or until the top is golden and a toothpick comes out clean when inserted in the deepest part of the cake.

Serve with fresh Brown Sugar Cream (see recipe below) and berries!

Brown Sugar Cream

INGREDIENTS

1 cup loosely packed dark brown sugar
2 cups sour cream
1 teaspoon vanilla extract

DIRECTIONS

Gently fold brown sugar into sour cream, making sure not to overmix. Add vanilla, and continue to carefully, slowly combine. With the brown sugar swirled throughout the cream, let stand in the refrigerator for a minimum of 1 hour. Remove, then fold to completely combine. Cream should still be thick and rich. Use this to top buttermilk pound cake, or serve with fresh strawberries.

Chocolate White Chocolate Chip Cookies

198

PREP TIME: 5 minutes **INACTIVE TIME:** 30 minutes
BAKE TIME: 10 to 12 minutes **YIELDS:** 2 dozen

Chocolate White Chocolate Chip Cookies

INGREDIENTS

1¼ cups all-purpose flour

½ cup unsweetened dark chocolate cocoa powder

1 teaspoon salt

1 teaspoon baking soda

1 cup butter, room temperature

2 eggs

¾ cup sugar

1 teaspoon vanilla extract

1 cup unpacked dark brown sugar

2 cups white chocolate chips

DIRECTIONS

Preheat the oven to 350°. Combine the flour, cocoa, salt, and baking soda in a bowl, mixing very well with a wire whisk. Set aside. Combine butter, eggs, sugar, vanilla, and dark brown sugar in a separate bowl. Slowly add the flour mixture and white chocolate chips. Mix until just combined. Drop dough in 1-ounce scoops onto a cookie sheet, and bake for 10 to 12 minutes or until just before set. Allow to cool for 10 minutes on the pan before removing to a wire rack.

PREP TIME: 10 minutes **YIELDS:** enough icing for one 9×13-inch cake or 12–16 cupcakes

Infamous Chocolate Sandwich Cookie Buttercream

> You know those trademark cookies that start with an O and end with an O? (There might be an R and an E in the middle somewhere.)

INGREDIENTS

- 1½ cups butter, softened
- 3 cups confectioners' sugar
- ½ teaspoon salt
- 2 tablespoons milk
- 1 package chocolate sandwich cookies

DIRECTIONS

In the bowl of a stand mixer, cream butter, sugar, salt, and milk until fluffy and creamy. Break chocolate cookies into pieces, all shapes and sizes. Fold cookies into the buttercream, and use to top a cake or cupcakes.

PREP TIME: 10–15 minutes **INACTIVE TIME:** 1 hour 40 minutes
BAKE TIME: 50 minutes **YIELDS:** 9 rolls

New-School Cinnamon Rolls

[I love homemade cinnamon rolls. These are so very tender and buttery!

SWEET MILK DOUGH

3 cups flour
1 cup whole milk, warmed
½ cup butter, softened
¼ sugar
1 egg
3 teaspoons bread machine yeast
1 teaspoon salt

FOR THE 9×13-INCH BAKING DISH

½ cup butter, softened
3 tablespoons maple syrup
½ cup brown sugar

CINNAMON ROLL FILLING

½ cup butter, softened but not completely melted
3 teaspoons ground cinnamon
1 cup brown sugar
1 teaspoon salt
Nuts or dried fruit, optional

DIRECTIONS

Put all dough ingredients into a bread machine and set on dough setting for 1 hour and 40 minutes. Check texture: if it's too dry, add milk 1 tablespoon at a time. If it's too moist, add flour 1 tablespoon at a time. This is moist dough; it'll be slightly sticky but should pull away from the sides of the bread machine. After you've reached the best consistency, just forget the dough for at least 2 hours. If you do not own a bread machine, mix all sweet dough ingredients by hand or in the bowl of a stand mixer for 7 minutes, until dough is smooth and somewhat tacky. Allow to rise at room temperature, covered, for 45 to 60 minutes.

When dough is finished, preheat oven to 350°, and prepare parchment-lined 9×13-inch baking dish (not optional) by smearing butter, maple syrup, and brown sugar in the bottom. Set aside.

Turn dough out onto a flour workspace, and gently form a large 20x10-inch rectangle. Spread melty butter over the dough, then sprinkle with cinnamon, brown sugar, and salt. This is a lovely opportunity to add nuts or dried fruit if you like.

Once the dough is decorated, roll it away from you into a tight, even coil. It doesn't have to be perfect!

Once rolled, slice into 9 even rolls. Place the rolls in prepared baking dish. Allow to rise for 30 minutes. Bake for 45 to 50 minutes or until rolls are golden brown and dough is cooked through. Pour Buttermilk Glaze on top of the rolls (see recipe page 229).

PREP TIME: 5 minutes **BAKE TIME:** 12 to 14 minutes **YIELDS** 2 dozen

Coconut Custard Macaroons

> These cookies are locally famous where I am from! Friends and coworkers request them all the time! I can remember when I first tried making them. Regular coconut macaroons were my all-time favorite, and I wanted to try them at home. Every recipe used only egg whites and sugar; condensed milk was in a few, but not many. Where was the butter? Where was the egg yolk? I didn't have time to whip soft peaks, thus the buttery egg-custard macaroon was born. It's been wowing folks since 2005.

INGREDIENTS

1 (17.5-ounce) package sweetened, shredded coconut
1 (14-ounce) can sweetened condensed milk
½ cup butter, melted
1 egg
1 teaspoon vanilla extract
¾ teaspoon sea salt

DIRECTIONS

Preheat the oven to 375°, and line a cookie sheet with parchment paper. Mix all the ingredients until the batter is completely mixed. Use an ice-cream scoop to distribute equal portions onto the cookie sheet. Bake until all edges and tops of cookies are golden brown, about 14 minutes. Depending on the weather, cookies might need a few additional minutes to bake. Let cookies set on cookie sheet for about 5 minutes, no more than 20, or they will stick! Transfer to serving dish or plate to continue cooling.

PREP TIME: 10 to 15 minutes **BAKE TIME:** 25 to 30 minutes
YIELDS: one 9×13-inch pan

Cream Cheese Pumpkin Pie Bars

THE CRUST
2 cups flour
½ cup sugar
1 teaspoon salt
1½ teaspoons baking powder
1 cup butter, melted

PUMPKIN FILLING
1 (29-ounce) can pure pumpkin or 3½ cups fresh roasted pumpkin flesh without the skin
1¼ cups dark brown sugar
1 cup cream
3 eggs
1 tablespoon vanilla extract
2 teaspoons pumpkin pie spice
1 teaspoon ground cinnamon
½ teaspoon salt

CREAM CHEESE SWIRL
1 (8-ounce) package cream cheese, room temperature
¾ cup confectioners' sugar

DIRECTIONS
Preheat the oven to 350°, and line a 9×13-inch pan with parchment paper. Whisk the dry ingredients for crust together in a mixing bowl. Pour melted butter into the flour mixture (it will look crumbly). Press the crust into the pan, and bake partially for 12 minutes until slightly set. (You're not looking for the crust to be completely cooked; only small patches beginning to turn golden.)

While the crust is baking, mix together all the ingredients for the pumpkin filling with a hand mixer or wire whisk. Set aside.

In another, smaller bowl, microwave cream cheese for 10 to 30 seconds until it's nicely melted. Add confectioners' sugar, and mix until the lumps have disappeared and it's smooth and creamy.

When the crust has finished partially baking, pour the pumpkin filling into the center. Quickly spread it evenly all over the crust. (It's perfectly fine if some of the crust moves under the weight of the pumpkin; it creates a tasty, thicker edge.)

Spoon the cream-cheese blend evenly over the pumpkin; I tend to get about 12 tablespoon dollops over the bars. Make sure to scrape every last bit on! Using your spoon, carefully drag through the cream-cheese dollops and pumpkin to create beautiful swirls. Do not over swirl, even though it is the best part.

Return to the oven for 20 to 30 minutes, and remove it just before the center is completely set. A small amount of wobble is fine, because your bars will continue to set as they cool. Slice into 12 large bars or 24 average ones. Try not to inhale the pan.

PREP TIME: 20 minutes **BAKE TIME:** 25 minutes
YIELDS: one 10-inch tart or one 14x4-inch rectangle tart, as shown

Frangipane Jam Tart

CRUST

¾ cup butter, softened
½ cup sugar
½ teaspoon kosher salt
1¾ cups flour

FRANGIPANE

1 cup almond flour or ground almond
¼ cup butter, melted
2 eggs
2 heaping tablespoons sugar
2 tablespoons all-purpose flour
1 teaspoon vanilla extract
½ teaspoon kosher salt
½ cup raspberry jam, warmed

DIRECTIONS

Preheat the oven to 350°. For the crust, cream butter, sugar, and salt until fluffy, and fold in the flour. It might be a touch crumbly, but that's just fine. Press the dough into tart pan. Bake for 15 minutes. Set aside, and allow to cool slightly.

For the filling, mix all the ingredients except the jam until smooth. Pour into your parbaked tart shell. Gently place at least 7 spoonfuls of warmed jam into the shell, taking great care not to let any of the dollops touch. Gently and lightly drag a fork through the jam to create lovely swirls! Bake for at least 25 minutes or until the tart has set and is slightly golden brown on top.

PREP TIME: 10 to 15 minutes **BAKE TIME:** 10 minutes
INACTIVE TIME: At least 4 hours **YIELDS:** one 9×13-inch pan

Citrus Tart

> I'm obsessed with curd! I love to add all kinds of citrus, not just lemon. Lemons and limes add a complexity that can't be beat!

CITRUS CURD

1 cup butter, softened
1¾ cups sugar
4 eggs
Juice and zest of 2 limes and 2 lemons (at least ½ to ¾ cup juice, including zest)

GRAHAM CRACKER CRUST

12 graham crackers, crushed
3 tablespoons butter, melted
1 tablespoon sugar
Pinch of salt
Fresh Whipped Cream (see recipe page 251)

DIRECTIONS

Mix the butter, sugar, and eggs in the bowl of an electric mixer. Pour in the citrus juice, then transfer to a nonstick saucepan and heat over medium heat until mixture becomes thick and passes the spoon-coat test. (When you run your finger along the back of the stirring spoon, the indentation does not run together.) Stir constantly and heat slowly, so you don't get scrambled eggs! Once the curd has fully thickened, place in a nonreactive bowl and set aside.

Preheat the oven to 350°. Pulse the graham crackers in a food processor until finely crumbed. Add the melted butter, sugar, and salt, and pulse 2 to 3 times more. Press the crust into the bottom of a 9-inch springform pan or 9-inch tart pan with removable sides. Bake for 10 minutes until golden. Cook on a wire rack for at least 1 hour. To assemble the tart, pour the prepared curd into the baked and cooled tart shell. Refrigerate for at least 3 hours before dolloping Fresh Whipped Cream on top. Chill another hour. Bring tart out at least 30 minutes before serving, and remove sides from the pan. Slice and serve!

PREP TIME: 10 to 15 minutes **BAKE TIME:** 12 to 18 minutes
YIELDS: 24 crackers

Homemade Graham Crackers

Do you ever wonder how to make something that's readily available at the grocery store? Lately, I find myself trying to make all kinds of pantry staples from scratch, and my mind is blown when it tastes the same or BETTER! That's how I feel about these Homemade Graham Crackers. I was thrilled to make a batch that not only tasted like I remember, but even turned out better than the boxed version with little effort. It's just like making a cookie! (Graham flour is actually just a special grind of wheat flour; it can be tricky to find, but whole-wheat pastry flour is in every grocery store and subs just fine!)

INGREDIENTS

1½ cups whole-wheat pastry flour or graham flour
½ cup all-purpose flour, plus extra for dusting
½ cup packed dark brown sugar
1 teaspoon ground cinnamon
½ teaspoon baking soda
½ teaspoon salt
½ cup butter, cold and cubed
¼ cup plus 2 tablespoons honey
¼ cup cold milk

DIRECTIONS

Preheat the oven to 350°. In the bowl of a stand mixer or using a hand mixer, mix all dry ingredients well. Add butter cubes, and mix until it resembles cornmeal, almost as if you're making a piecrust. Add honey and milk, and mix until it just forms into a ball. (This will be slightly moist dough.) Turn the dough out onto a floured surface, and roll out in a rectangular shape. Use a butter knife or square cookie cutter to create 3x3-inch squares, large enough to house a giant overfilled s'more! Bake on a cookie sheet for 12 to 18 minutes. This recipe makes 24 crackers.

Just in case you haven't had the pleasure of making a s'more: Place at least 2 small squares of chocolate on a graham cracker. If you don't have a freshly fire-roasted marshmallow, microwave a marshmallow on the chocolate-covered cracker for around 10 seconds. Sandwich another cracker on top of the marshmallow and chocolate to create the gooiest treat that everyone will love! I hope you enjoy these as much as my family does!

PREP TIME: 5 minutes **INACTIVE TIME:** 4 hours
YIELDS: 12 4-ounce popsicles

Creamy Coconut Apple Strawberry Popsicles

> The possibilities are endless here; you can easily use this recipe as a jumping-off point for any frozen combo.

INGREDIENTS

- 1 (12-ounce) can frozen apple-juice concentrate
- 1 cup fresh fruit (I used strawberries)
- 1 cup coconut cream (from the can)

DIRECTIONS

Combine all the ingredients in a blender, and pulse a few times. (I like my fruit to retain a bit of shape.) Carefully pour into freezer-proof popsicle molds or ice-cube trays. Place in freezer in a level area, and freeze for a minimum of 4 hours, or up to 2 days. Enjoy within a week for best flavor.

This recipe makes 12 popsicles in a standard at-home popsicle maker; you also could use ice-cube trays or blend it in smoothies! (You will have some popsicle base leftover; you could always just drink the base with a few ice cubes, too! It's heavenly.)

Dark Chocolate Salted Almond Bark

214

PREP TIME: 5 to 10 minutes **INACTIVE TIME:** 60 minutes
YIELDS: one 9×13-inch pan

Dark Chocolate Salted Almond Bark

If you can breathe, you can make this easy treat! I was a fan of the salty-sweets craze long before it was a fad. I think 3 million other women would attest to the love of salty-sweet snack!

INGREDIENTS

16 ounces good dark chocolate pieces
2 cups roasted almonds
½ teaspoon kosher salt

DIRECTIONS

Line a cookie sheet with parchment paper. For the almonds, you can use any style you like, but I prefer 2 cups raw almonds, which I roast on a dry cookie sheet at 350° until they're fragrant. (Pay careful attention, as the oil in the nuts is very delicate and can go from perfectly roasted to burned in a matter of seconds.) Cool the almonds completely. Microwave the chocolate pieces in a large mixing bowl at 50 percent power in 30-second bursts until completely melted and smooth. Add the almonds, and mix thoroughly and quickly into the chocolate. Use a plastic spatula to transfer the chocolate and almonds free-form onto parchment paper. Quickly and lightly sprinkle salt on top. Refrigerate for about 1 hour or until the chocolate is set. Break into large pieces, and enjoy.

PREP TIME: 15 minutes **BAKE TIME:** 35 to 40 minutes
INACTIVE TIME: 2 hours **YIELDS:** 4 4-ounce ramekins

Espresso Crusted Crème Brûlée

> I didn't have a torch to caramelize these guys, but I didn't let that stop me! Just sprinkle Sugar/Espresso Mix on top, and cook in the broiler on high for around 1 minute. Watch them very carefully; they burn quickly! The espresso granules make for an even smokier crunch, and it's pretty much to die for!

INGREDIENTS
2 cups heavy cream
1 vanilla bean, split lengthwise
4 large egg yolks
¼ cup plus 1 tablespoon sugar
Hot water

SUGAR/ESPRESSO MIX
½ cup light brown sugar
2 tablespoons super-finely ground espresso

DIRECTIONS
Heat the cream with the vanilla bean in a medium, heavy-bottomed, nonreactive saucepan over medium-low heat for 15 minutes, stirring to ensure the cream does not burn. Do not let it boil. Remove from the heat, and let stand for 15 minutes. Discard the vanilla bean.

Preheat the oven to 300°. Beat the yolks in a large bowl with an electric mixer on high speed for 5 minutes until light and fluffy. Gradually beat in the sugar. Add half the cream mixture, a little at a time, to the egg mixture, whisking until well blended. Pour the egg mixture into the remaining cream mixture. Mix thoroughly. Pour custard into 4 medium ramekins or custard cups. Place the dishes in a large baking pan. Pour enough hot water into the pan to come halfway up the sides of the ramekins.

Bake for 35 to 40 minutes or until the mixture is set in the center (it should still wiggle when shaken). Carefully remove the dishes from the baking pan. Let cool to room temperature, and refrigerate for at least 2 hours.

Sprinkle an even layer of Sugar/Espresso Mix over each Crème Brûlée, covering completely. (I use about 1 tablespoon each.) To caramelize the sugar, place custards on a baking sheet and heat in preheated broiler on high for only 1 to 2 minutes. You want the sugar to bubble but not turn too black. Serve right away. The sugar won't retain its crunch, but these do keep well in the fridge for up to 1 day after the sugar has been broiled.

PREP TIME: 15 minutes **BAKE TIME:** 12 to 15 minutes
YIELDS: 8 to 10 scones

Cream Scones with Warm Honey & Fresh Strawberry Mash

[These scones make a lovely base for strawberry shortcake, too!

INGREDIENTS

2¼ cups flour, spooned and leveled
½ cup sugar
1 tablespoon baking powder
½ teaspoon salt
½ cup butter, cold and cut into tiny pieces
¾ cup heavy whipping cream
½ teaspoon vanilla extract
1 egg, lightly beaten
Heavy cream and raw sugar for topping, optional
Melted butter and raw honey for topping, optional

DIRECTIONS

Preheat the oven to 375°. Combine the dry ingredients in a bowl, and mix thoroughly with a wire whisk. Cut the cold butter in with a pastry knife or fork. Make a well in the center of the flour mixture, and add cream, vanilla, and egg. Mix by cutting through the center and folding until the batter has just come together. Turn out onto a floured surface, and form into an 8-inch circle. Cut the circle in half, then cut each half in half again, until you have 8 perfect little triangles. Arrange triangles on a baking sheet, and bake for around 15 minutes or until golden brown on top. (As an option, brush the top of each scone with a bit of heavy cream, and sprinkle with raw sugar before baking.)

Strawberry Mash

1 cup fresh super-ripe strawberries
2 tablespoons sugar
Pinch of salt

DIRECTIONS

Sometimes jam can be a bit too sweet when I want to enjoy the fresh berries of the season. But this mash is simple and balanced: just mash the berries with sugar and salt. Normally, strawberries at the peak of the season will smash quite nicely with just a fork, but you always can chop them up first. Spoon onto warm scones; add a little melted butter and warm honey, and you've got a party!

Lemon Curd

INGREDIENTS

4 eggs
½ cup butter, softened
1 cup sugar
Juice and zest of 2 small lemons (or 1 large one)

DIRECTIONS

Combine the eggs, butter, and sugar in the bowl of a stand mixer or using an electric hand mixer, and mix thoroughly. Add lemon juice and zest, and pour into a nonreactive medium saucepan. Heat on medium until the mixture thickens into curd, about 10 minutes. If it looks separated at first, that's fine; it will come together. Stir constantly, and do not let it get too hot, or the eggs will scramble! Cool to room temperature before using. This lasts in the fridge up to 3 days. Bring to room temperature before serving.

PREP TIME: 10 minutes **BAKE TIME:** 25 to 30 minutes
YIELDS: two 8-inch round pans

Strawberry Lemonade Cake

This cake is so lovely and unfussy, I don't trim the layers.

INGREDIENTS

1½ cups superfine white sugar
1 cup butter, softened
1 teaspoon vanilla extract
Juice and zest of 1 lemon
1 teaspoon salt
4 eggs
1¼ cups cream
3 cups flour
1 tablespoon baking powder
Lemon Curd, cooled (see recipe page 220)
Fresh Whipped Cream (see recipe page 251)
2 cups sliced strawberries, for topping

DIRECTIONS

Preheat the oven to 350°, and line the bottom of 2 8-inch round pans with parchment paper. Butter the sides of the pans. Beat the sugar and butter in one bowl until light and fluffy. Add the vanilla, lemon juice and zest, and salt, and mix gently. Mix the eggs and cream in a separate bowl. Mix the flour and baking powder in a third bowl. In three alternating additions, add the flour/baking powder mixture to the butter/sugar, then the cream, gently folding after each addition. Mix until just incorporated. Divide the batter between the cake pans, and bake for 25 to 30 minutes or until a pick comes out clean. Cool cakes completely before filling.

Place one cooled cake layer on serving pedestal. Add ⅓ of Lemon Curd and ⅓ of Fresh Whipped Cream. Top with second cooled cake layer, and add another ⅓ each of curd and cream, smoothing in a rustic fashion, and top with 2 cups sliced, juicy strawberries. Serve by slicing and adding an extra spoon of the reserved curd and whipped cream!

To make this cake extra fun, top with whipped cream and strawberries!

SWEETS

PREP TIME: 5 to 10 minutes **COOK TIME:** 30 to 45 minutes
YIELDS: one 9×13 pan

Plum Crumble

INGREDIENTS

7 to 10 black plums (depending on size), sliced to yield 6 to 7 cups of fruit

¾ cup sugar

Butter (for the baking dish)

CRUMBLE TOPPING

2 cups all-purpose flour

1 cup butter

1 cup sugar

½ cup brown sugar

1 teaspoon baking powder

1 teaspoon salt

DIRECTIONS

Preheat the oven to 350°, and liberally butter a 9×13-inch glass baking dish. Arrange the sliced plums in the dish, and sprinkle the sugar over the top. Combine all topping ingredients in a separate mixing bowl, and mash with a fork until you get crumbly well-mixed bits, ranging in size from a pea to an almond. Sprinkle crumble mixture over the plums, and bake for at least 45 minutes or until the crumble is bubbling and golden brown on top.

PREP TIME: 5 to 10 minutes **INACTIVE TIME:** 3 hours **YIELDS:** 1 pie

Peanut Butter Ice Box Pie

FILLING
1 (8-ounce) package cream cheese, softened
1 cup smooth peanut butter
½ cup confectioner's sugar
1 teaspoon vanilla extract
½ teaspoon salt
2 cups prepared vanilla pudding
3 cups Fresh Whipped Cream (see recipe page 251)
½ cup toasted salted peanuts

CRUST
15 shortbread cookies
1 stick butter, melted

DIRECTIONS
Whip the cream cheese and peanut butter in the bowl of a stand mixer on low speed for 3 minutes, slowly increasing the speed to medium. Scrape down the sides of the bowl, and add the sugar, vanilla, and salt. Mix until smooth. Slowly add the pudding, and mix until it's completely come together.

Meanwhile, crush shortbread cookies and mix with melted butter. Press into a 9- or 10-inch pie dish. Pour peanut-butter filling into the prepared crust. Let stand in the refrigerator for 3 hours.

Gently spread Fresh Whipped Cream over the pie, and sprinkle salted peanuts on top!

SWEETS

Pistachio Orange Shortbread Cookies

PREP TIME: 5 to 10 minutes **BAKE TIME:** 10–12 minutes
YIELDS: 2 dozen cookies

Pistachio Orange Shortbread Cookies

Crumbly buttery and quite tasty! Shortbread cookies are the most versatile and crowd-pleasing cookie beside the king chocolate chip! Almost any flavors can be added to make this your very own recipe.

INGREDIENTS

1 cup butter, room temperature
¾ cup confectioners' sugar
¼ teaspoon salt
1 teaspoon vanilla extract
1 tablespoon freshly grated orange zest
2 cups all-purpose flour
½ cup toasted, chopped pistachios

DIRECTIONS

Cream butter, sugar, salt, vanilla, and orange zest until smooth, then fold in flour and pistachios. Roll the mixture into 2 logs, wrap in parchment, and let rest in the refrigerator for 2 hours. About 20 minutes before you're ready to bake the cookies, preheat the oven to 350°, and line a cookie sheet with parchment paper. Slice the cookies about ¼-inch thick, and arrange on the cookie sheet. Bake for 10 to 12 minutes or until the cookies are golden!

Buttermilk Blueberry Muffins with Lemon Shortbread Crumbles & Buttermilk Glaze

PREP TIME: 5 to 10 minutes **BAKE TIME:** 20 to 25 minutes
YIELDS: one mini Bundt pan or 12 to 16 muffins

Buttermilk Blueberry Muffins with Lemon Shortbread Crumbles & Buttermilk Glaze

BLUEBERRY MUFFINS

1½ cups flour (plus 2 tablespoons set aside)

1 cup sugar

¾ cup almond flour

3 teaspoons baking powder

1 teaspoon kosher salt

¾ cup buttermilk

Juice of 1 lemon (save the zest for the crumble top)

½ cup melted butter

1 egg

2 cups fresh blueberries

LEMON SHORTBREAD CRUMBLE TOPPING

¾ cup flour

½ cup sugar

⅓ cup butter, softened

Zest of 1 lemon

Buttermilk Glaze

1 cup confectioners' sugar

2 to 3 tablespoons buttermilk

DIRECTIONS

Mix and set aside.

DIRECTIONS

Preheat the oven to 350°. Mix the dry ingredients together in a large bowl. Make a well in the center, and add all wet ingredients. Fold the batter into itself until it's just mixed. Toss blueberries with 2 tablespoons flour just to coat them; this will keep them from sinking to the bottom of the batter. Gently fold berries into batter. Do not overmix this one; you want those berries to burst during baking, not in your batter bowl.

If you are using liners, fill each one ¾ full with batter, and place about 1 tablespoon of Lemon Shortbread Crumble Topping on top of each. This made about 12 heaping muffins for me, but I overfilled mine; you should get about 16 muffins. Bake for 20 to 25 minutes or until they are golden and puffed up and a pick comes out clean!

Once they have cooled slightly, drizzle Buttermilk Glaze all over the top!

I baked these guys in a mini Bundt pan so they would resemble donuts! They sure were fun to eat. Noah loved them, and he loved helping. The shortbread topping is really unexpected and basically what's been missing from blueberry everything for as long as blueberries have been around! I think next time I will go for a large muffin tin with liners or a 9×13-inch cake pan for a coffee cake. They are light, airy, and full of flavor.

SWEETS 229

Piecrust Tips
TIPS FOR AMAZING, FLAKY, LIGHT CRUST EVERY TIME:
Chill dough (see recipe page 233) for at least 30 minutes or up to 4 hours.

Allow the crust to sit at room temperature for about 10 minutes before you roll it out. Flatten pie dough into a disc (or 2 discs for a double-crust pie) before chilling; this allows for easier rollout.

Shortening makes for even flakier layers. Don't overwork it. Rustic, or messy, always wins.

Additional Fun Tips

Use dough scraps for a crumbly topping shortcut.

Add a tablespoon of lemon juice to overripe fruit intended for pie filling to bring back a fresh, tart taste.

Skip flour or thickeners in underripe fruit so you get a bit of juice in your pie. A sprinkle of salt in pie filling evens out the flavor profile and adds pop.

PREP TIME: 10 to 15 minutes **INACTIVE TIME:** 30 minutes
BAKE TIME: 60 minutes **YIELDS:** one 9-inch pie

Blueberry Pie

> I have been making pie fillings without a recipe since I was about 12 years old. My mom always said ¼ cup of sugar and ¼ cup of flour to 4 to 5 cups ripe sweet fruit, and ½ cup of sugar if the fruit was tart. Dot the top with butter up to ½ cup. Put a top crust or crumble on top! I employed this when making the blueberry pie!

INGREDIENTS

4 cups blueberries
¼ cup sugar
¼ cup flour
½ cup butter

DIRECTIONS

Preheat the oven to 350°. Mix everything except the butter in a bowl, and pour into piecrust. Dot the top with all that tasty butter. I used the leftover crust trimmings to make a crumbly top. Bake for about 60 minutes on a baking sheet to catch overflow. Cool, and enjoy!

Butter Pie Dough

I definitely cannot take any credit for making a piecrust recipe! You can't mess up or add to perfection! This perfect crust is a French cooking benchmark.

2½ cups all-purpose flour
1 cup cold butter, cubed
1 tablespoon sugar
1 teaspoon salt
¼ to ½ cup ice water

DIRECTIONS

Mix the first four ingredients in the bowl of a stand mixer or using a pastry cutter until it's crumbly and resembles large or coarse ground cornmeal. While the mixer is on the lowest setting, slowly add just enough ice water to bring your dough together. Transfer the pie dough onto a large piece of plastic wrap, and form into a disc. Wrap tightly, and chill for 30 minutes or up to 3 days! Allow pastry to sit at room temperature for about 10 minutes before rolling out on a floured surface.

PREP TIME: 10 to 15 minutes **BAKE TIME:** 45 to 60 minutes
YIELDS: one 9-inch pie

Spiced Caramel Apple Pie

> I never throw away a scrap of dough! Simply lay extras on the baking sheet, and sprinkle with cinnamon and sugar! Also, if your crust edges begin to darken, tent with foil to finish baking. For a glossy bakery crust, beat 1 egg with 1 tablespoon water, and brush over the crust before baking. Then sprinkle with cinnamon and sugar!

INGREDIENTS

5 to 6 Granny Smith apples (or any tart apple), peeled and thinly sliced
1¼ cups dark brown sugar
½ cup butter
1 tablespoon pumpkin pie spice
1 teaspoon kosher salt
2 tablespoons flour
Butter Pie Dough (see recipe page 233)

DIRECTIONS

Combine first five ingredients in a medium saucepan, and cook for 10 minutes over medium heat until the apples begin to lose a bit of their crunch. (I love using pumpkin pie spice in apple pie you get four or five sweet, warm spices in one ingredient!) Remove from heat, sprinkle flour over the apples, and mix thoroughly.

Preheat the oven to 350°. Divide the pie dough in two. Roll half out for the bottom crust, and place in a 9-inch pie dish. Pour the filling in. Roll the other half of the dough out into a 10×10-inch square, and slice into 8 strips. Lay 4 strips across the pie lengthwise, then make a 90-degree turn and lay the other 4 the opposite way. No weaving. Who's got time for weaving? Use your fingers to pinch and crimp the edges of the lattice strips to edge the crust. Place pie on a lined baking sheet, and bake for about 60 minutes.

PREP TIME: 5 to 10 minutes **BAKE TIME:** 45 to 60 minutes
YIELDS: one 9-inch pie

Strawberry Lime Pie

INGREDIENTS

Butter Pie Dough (see recipe page 233)
4 to 5 cups fresh strawberries, sliced
½ to ¾ cup sugar, depending on berries' sweetness
Juice and zest of 1 lime
¼ cup flour
1 teaspoon salt

DIRECTIONS

Roll out pastry, and press into the bottom of a 9-inch deep pie dish or a 10-inch tart pan that has been lined with parchment paper. Trim the excess dough, and break it up to add to the top of the pie (you should have about 1 cup of scraps). Preheat the oven to 350°. Lightly mix the remaining ingredients in a large bowl. Pour the mixture into the shell, and dot the top with reserved dough bits. Place the pie on a baking sheet, and bake for at least 45 minutes or until the pastry is golden and the strawberries have bubbled and thickened to resemble jam. If in doubt, always bake a pie a touch longer!

PREP TIME: 5 to 10 minutes **BAKE TIME:** 45 to 60 minutes
YIELDS: one 9×13-inch pan

Rhubarb & Raspberry Crisp

> I have a confession: I had never worked with rhubarb until this year! I had a rhubarb pie once that was so bitter, I never took interest in trying it or cooking with it on my own again! My sister purchased some at the market and didn't have time to cook with it, so without even consulting a recipe, I threw together a basic crisp. It was anything but basic; it was one of the best crisps I had ever tasted! How had rhubarb eluded me all these years? I had seriously been missing out. Rhubarb is tangy and reminds me of a lighter-in-texture Granny Smith apple with an almost celery-like texture. It bakes up so beautifully in almost any pie, crisp, or tart. Now I know!

FILLING

4 cups sliced rhubarb (about 3 large stalks)
¼ cup all-purpose flour
1½ cups sugar
2 cups fresh raspberries

OAT TOPPING

2 cups oats
½ cup dark brown sugar
2 tablespoons all-purpose flour
1 teaspoon salt
1 teaspoon vanilla extract
½ cup butter, melted

DIRECTIONS

Preheat oven to 350°. Liberally butter a 9×13-inch glass baking dish. Toss the rhubarb with the flour and sugar in a mixing bowl to evenly coat. Pour mix into the bottom of baking dish. Sprinkle with raspberries.

Combine the first five topping ingredients in a separate bowl. Add melted butter, and combine. Pour oat mixture on top of the fruit, and dot with additional butter if you desire! (I almost always do!) Bake at least 45 minutes, until the fruit is bubbly and fork-tender. Let cool for at least 20 minutes, and serve warm with vanilla ice cream.

Bread Pudding French Toast with Strawberry Syrup

238

PREP TIME: 5 minutes **COOK TIME:** 15 to 20 minutes
YIELDS: 10 to 12 slices

Bread Pudding French Toast with Strawberry Syrup

INGREDIENTS

1 loaf brioche, cut into 1-inch slices (about 10 slices)

4 eggs

3 cups milk

1 tablespoon ground cinnamon

1 teaspoon vanilla extract

½ cup packed brown sugar

½ teaspoon salt

1 cube butter, softened, for frying

¾ cup confectioners' sugar, for dusting

Strawberry Syrup (see recipe page 187)

DIRECTIONS

Slice brioche, lay slices on a tray, and set aside. Beat eggs, milk, cinnamon, vanilla, sugar, and salt in a large mixing bowl until the eggs no longer hold any elasticity, about 4 minutes. Meanwhile, heat a large skillet to medium, and add 1 tablespoon butter to the pan. Dredge 2 slices of bread at a time, and allow them to soak in the custard for at least 30 seconds. Lay 2 soaked slices of bread in the pan at once. Brown the French toast for at least 3 minutes before flipping. (If the pan is too hot, you will burn the bread before a golden crust forms, so pay careful attention and adjust the heat accordingly.) Flip the bread, and cook for an additional 2 minutes or until it's done! Add a fresh pat of butter to the pan before each slice is fried. Repeat until you've used all your bread and custard. To finish, sprinkle with confectioners' sugar, and drizzle with fresh strawberry syrup.

PREP TIME: 10 minutes **BAKE TIME:** 12 to 18 minutes
YIELDS: 8 tarts

Stone Fruit Chèvre Tarts

INGREDIENTS

- 1 package store-bought puff pastry
- 4 ounces cream cheese, softened
- 2 ounces chèvre or other mild, creamy goat cheese
- ¾ cup confectioners' sugar
- ½ teaspoon salt
- ½ teaspoon vanilla extract
- 3 to 4 ripe peaches or nectarines, each sliced into at least 10 wedges
- 1 egg, beaten
- 1 cup apricot jam (optional)

DIRECTIONS

Thaw puff pastry according to package directions. Flour a clean counter or board, and lay out pastry. Cut sheets into four, and lay on a cookie sheet.

Preheat the oven to 400°. Combine cream cheese, chèvre, sugar, salt, and vanilla in the bowl of a stand mixer, and mix until it comes together. Spoon 1 to 2 tablespoons of the cheese mixture into the center of each pastry. Lay at least 4 or 5 slices of fruit on the cheese mixture, and brush the edges of the pastry with egg. Bake for 12 to 18 minutes or until the pastry has puffed and is golden brown.

In a saucepan over medium heat, melt apricot jam. Remove from heat. Spoon or brush over warm pastry. Serve immediately!

Tart Cherry Dark Chocolate Granola Bars

PREP TIME: 5 minutes **BAKE TIME:** 20 minutes
YIELDS: one 9×13-inch pan

Tart Cherry Dark Chocolate Granola Bars

INGREDIENTS

1 cup unpacked brown sugar

¾ cup almond butter

½ cup honey or corn syrup

½ cup melted butter

½ teaspoon salt

2 cups old-fashioned oats

1 cup chopped dark chocolate

1 cup dried tart cherries

¾ cup shredded sweetened coconut

½ cup wheat germ

DIRECTIONS

Preheat the oven to 350°, and butter a 9×13-inch pan. Combine the first five ingredients, and mix well. Add the remaining ingredients and mix again. Press into the pan, and bake for 20 minutes. Let cool completely before slicing, or they will crumble. They're heavenly with vanilla ice cream!

PREP TIME: 5 to 10 minutes **BAKE TIME:** 8 to 10 minutes
YIELDS: 16 to 18 cookies

Sticky Marshmallow Toffee Cookies with Black Hawaiian Sea Salt

> Making these cookies was epic: I am an avid experimenter in the baking kitchen, and when my mother came back from a trip to Hawaii with black sea salt in tow, I flipped with joy. Black salt? Yes, crunchy, mineral-rich black salt. It's made by mixing lava charcoal and salt in some fabulous way to create a soft salt that lends a beautiful bite and slow finish to any dish. In honor of the salt craze in the sweets world, these gooey cookies needed just a hint of crunchy salt to be perfect. They are, quite possibly, one of the best I've ever made.

INGREDIENTS

¼ cup white sugar
½ cup dark brown sugar
1 cup butter, softened
1 teaspoon vanilla extract
2 eggs, room temperature
2¼ cups flour
½ teaspoon baking soda
2 cups mini marshmallows
1½ cups chocolate chips
1 tablespoon black Hawaiian sea salt, fleur de sel or any soft-tasting salt, for sprinkling

DIRECTIONS

Preheat oven to 350°. Line baking sheets with parchment. (You mustn't skip this step. Hot marshmallow acts like glue, and without it, your cookies will not release properly once cooled.) Mix sugars, butter, and vanilla until it's just come together. Add eggs one at a time. Mix until just combined; don't overmix at any point in this cookie game. Add flour and baking soda, and mix gently until about halfway combined. Add marshmallows and chocolate chips, and mix, again, just until it's come together.

Spoon cookies, about 2 tablespoons of batter each, onto lined sheet, and bake for 8 minutes. (They need no more than 10 minutes of baking, but check at 8.) Remove, sprinkle with salt, and allow to cool completely on the pan. Due to the cookies' gooey nature, I cut squares of parchment and layer it between cookies for storing if they make it that far!

Simple and From Scratch

I always want to push the envelope, to find the best way, to challenge the way it's always been done.

The right dressing, cream, or sauce can really transform a dish from great to amazing. During our restaurant days, people absolutely loved the from-scratch *everything* when it came to dressings. You'd never catch a store-bought bottle hiding out. Until I started working at Minoela, I had no idea that you could make real ranch dressing without a packet of powdery stuff! Don't be offended; I still have love for that buttermilk packet. But my very favorite ranch dressing is made with real buttermilk, fresh garlic, loads of fresh herbs, sour cream, and freshly cracked black pepper. There is nothing quite like it. But that's life, right? Years pass, and you find yourself doing a certain something one certain way…until, one day, you are shown a better way of achieving the same end. Suddenly, it turns out that what was good enough isn't the best any longer. I always want to push the envelope, to find the best way, to challenge the way it's always been done. This chapter is filled with items you can easily buy already prepared, but if you'd just try them from scratch, you might never again find yourself dropping them into your shopping cart. Enjoy all these simple and delicious dressings, sauces, and toppings. May they make your meals *infinitely* better and all the more tasty!

PREP TIME: 5 minutes **COOK TIME:** 4 to 5 minutes **INACTIVE TIME:** 30 minutes **YIELDS:** about 12 ounces

Herbed Fresh Ricotta Cheese

INGREDIENTS
3 cups whole milk
2 cups cream
1 teaspoon salt
¼ cup lemon juice
1 cup diced chives
½ cup chopped parsley
½ cup shredded parmesan cheese
1 teaspoon black pepper

DIRECTIONS
Bring milk, cream, and salt to a simmer. Once you've reached 190° (you can tell you've come to a proper temperature or simmer when tiny bubbles form just along the rim of your pan, or by using a thermometer), turn off the heat, and add the lemon juice. Allow to sit for about 4 minutes, stirring only once.

Wet a piece of cheesecloth and fold so that you have at least two layers. Place the cloth inside a colander, and set the colander inside a larger bowl or pot to catch the whey. Pour milk and lemon-juice mixture into the cheesecloth-lined colander. Allow to drain for at least 30 minutes.

Roll fresh ricotta into a mixing bowl, and add the rest of the ingredients. Mix completely, and refrigerate. This mixture lasts about 5 days covered in the fridge.

PREP TIME: 5 minutes **COOK TIME:** 10 to 15 minutes **YIELDS:** 16 ounces

Lemon Simple Syrup

> This is perfect for any drink mixer!

INGREDIENTS
1¼ cups sugar
1 cup water
Juice of 1 lemon
Zest strips of 2 lemons (only the bright yellow part)

DIRECTIONS
For zest strips, use a sharp vegetable peeler to remove only that thin, beautiful lemon zest in perfect long strips, no white pith. Combine all the ingredients in a saucepan, and bring to a simmer until the sugar is completely dissolved. Cool to room temperature, and store in the fridge for up to 7 days for all your party needs!

PREP TIME: 5 minutes **YIELDS:** 2½ cups

Vanilla Bean Pouring Cream

INGREDIENTS
½ cup sugar
Seeds of 1 vanilla-bean pod
2 cups heavy cream
1 teaspoon vanilla extract

DIRECTIONS
In a cold bowl, whisk sugar, vanilla seeds, and cream. You're not making whipped cream, but you do want the cream to thicken slightly. Cover tightly, and keep in the refrigerator until it's time to use over warm crisps, crumbles, or pound cake. Keeps refrigerated for up to 3 days.

Salted Toffee Sauce

PREP TIME: 5 minutes **COOK TIME:** 5 to 10 minutes **YIELDS:** 16 ounces

Salted Toffee Sauce

This sauce is wonderful on French toast or ice cream and tastes heavenly. My sister and her kiddos came up to visit on a warm summer night, and I happened to have a half-gallon of vanilla ice cream in the freezer and fresh raspberries in the fridge. The only thing missing was sticky toffee sauce! I had no butter, only cream. Go figure! I substituted, and it was a happy mistake, as the sauce was light and creamy. Perfect addition to our sundaes!

INGREDIENTS

1½ cup dark brown sugar
1 teaspoon salt
¾ cup heavy cream

DIRECTIONS

Combine the sugar, salt, and cream in a heavy-bottomed saucepan over medium heat. Stir constantly with a wooden spoon, and heat until just bubbling, so all the sugar has dissolved into the cream. The sauce will thicken slightly. Pour into a glass container with a pour spout. Cool for about 10 minutes, and douse whatever's waiting for it!

PREP TIME: 4 to 6 minutes **YIELDS:** 4 cups

Fresh Whipped Cream

INGREDIENTS

2 cups cold heavy cream
¼ cup plus 1 tablespoon sugar
1 teaspoon vanilla extract
½ teaspoon salt

DIRECTIONS

Whip all the ingredients at medium speed until soft peaks form, about 4 to 6 minutes. Careful to not overmix, as you could start to make butter!

PREP TIME: 30 minutes **COOK TIME:** 15 to 25 minutes
YIELDS: 6 8-ounce jars

Plum Preserves

In early September, the Italian plums begin to drop, and it's a sign the small, sweet fruit is ready for plucking! After reading several recipes, I settled on making my own preserves to remind me of autumn and all its glory. I make a buttery shortbread to spread this on! The warm spices are comforting, and the tart, tangy fruit is a welcome addition to any ice cream or fresh scone.

INGREDIENTS

5 cups pitted Italian black plums
1 cup chopped walnuts or pecans
¾ cup chopped dried dates
½ cup apple juice
½ cup dried cranberries
¼ cup fresh lemon juice
¼ cup orange juice
1 teaspoon ground cinnamon
1 teaspoon orange zest
1 teaspoon pumpkin pie spice
¼ teaspoon kosher salt
3 cups loosely packed dark brown sugar

DIRECTIONS

Combine all the ingredients except sugar in a large pot, and bring to a rolling boil. Continue to cook for 5 to 7 minutes until all fruit is tender and a rich purple color has developed. Add sugar. Return to a hard boil for 10 minutes. Drop a teaspoon of jam on a plate, and pop in the fridge for 1 minute. Then run your finger through the preserves; if the line does not run back together, your jam is ready to be canned, frozen, or given to friends and enjoyed. It lasts up to 2 weeks in the fridge if it's not given a water bath.

PREP TIME: 5 minutes **YIELDS:** 12 ounces

Apple Cider Honey Mustard

> This tangy dressing is amazing as a marinade applied before grilling fish or chicken. I love it on good ol' salad. Enjoy it on everything!

INGREDIENTS
¼ cup apple cider vinegar
¼ cup good honey
¼ cup your favorite prepared mustard
½ teaspoon salt
¼ teaspoon freshly ground black pepper
½ cup good olive oil

DIRECTIONS
Combine all the ingredients except the olive oil. Whisk until smooth and honey is completely dissolved into the mustard. Slowly stream olive oil into the mixture to create an emulsification. (That's a fancy way of saying the dressing will begin to thicken and come together.)

PREP TIME: 5 minutes **COOK TIME:** 30 minutes **YIELDS:** 8 to 10 ounces

Quick Balsamic & Tomato Jam

This is quick and impressive; once this gooey golden goodness is finished, you can smear it on anything: burgers, salmon, or messy egg sandwiches!

INGREDIENTS

2 to 3 cups cherry tomatoes, halved
½ cup balsamic vinegar
2 tablespoons olive oil
1 teaspoon freshly ground black pepper
1 teaspoon kosher salt

DIRECTIONS

Cook the whole shebang over medium heat for about 30 minutes. It will reduce by half and turn thick and amazing. Stir constantly, and if you notice it getting too dry or sticky, reduce heat.

PREP TIME: 5 minutes **COOK TIME:** 15 minutes **YIELDS:** 4 cups

Quick Sauerkraut

INGREDIENTS

5 to 6 cups shredded green cabbage (1 medium head)

1 cup apple cider vinegar

½ cup water

2 to 3 tablespoons kosher salt

2 tablespoons sugar

2 teaspoons freshly ground black pepper

DIRECTIONS

Bring all to a simmer over medium-high heat for 15 minutes, and you've got tangy, amazing fresh sauerkraut!

PREP TIME: 5 minutes **YIELDS:** 3 cups

Garlic Cheddar Butter

This is great on grilled corn and perfect on our Garlic & Cheddar Corn Bread (see recipe page 81)!

INGREDIENTS

1½ cups shredded cheddar cheese
1 cup room-temperature salted butter
3 tablespoons chopped fresh parsley
2 cloves fresh garlic, finely chopped
Pinch of freshly ground black pepper
Pinch of salt

DIRECTIONS

Simply mix everything at once, by hand, in a mixing bowl. Once the butter is combined, transfer to a small serving dish, and refrigerate up to 2 days. It will get stronger the longer it sits. It's got a very garlicky bite, so reduce the garlic to 1 clove if you like a softer garlic taste.

PREP TIME: 5 minutes **YIELDS:** 2 cups

Sun-Dried Tomato Pesto

INGREDIENTS

¼ cup Marcona almonds
1 tablespoon toasted pepitas (optional)
½ cup oil-packed sun-dried tomatoes
¾ cup good parmesan cheese
3 cups spinach
1 clove fresh garlic, minced
Juice of 1 lemon
¾ cup olive oil
1 teaspoon freshly cracked black pepper
Sprinkle of sea salt

DIRECTIONS

Combine ingredients in a food processor in the order they're listed. Pulse until a smooth, loose pesto comes together. If you need a bit more oil, just add a touch more! Smear this treat on bread or fish, or use as an accompaniment to Brie and cured olives with tomatoes.

PREP TIME: 5 minutes **INACTIVE TIME:** 1 hour **YIELDS:** 2½ cups

Buttermilk Ranch Dressing

INGREDIENTS

1 cup sour cream

1 cup mayonnaise

½ cup buttermilk

½ cup half-and-half or whole milk

1 teaspoon each of the following: dried basil, dried chives, dried rosemary (double the amounts if using fresh herbs)

1 teaspoon granulated garlic

1 teaspoon kosher salt

1 teaspoon onion powder

½ teaspoon freshly cracked black pepper

DIRECTIONS

Whisk all the ingredients together; add more milk or buttermilk for desired consistency. Make sure to taste for flavor. After about 1 hour in the fridge, it begins to marry beautifully. You'll be pouring this over everything!

PREP TIME: 5 minutes **YIELDS:** 1½ cups

Sun-Dried Tomato Aioli

INGREDIENTS

1 cup your favorite mayonnaise
½ cup chopped, oil-packed sun-dried tomatoes
1 teaspoon fresh lemon juice
½ teaspoon freshly cracked black pepper

DIRECTIONS

Whisk together all the ingredients. It's really that easy! Variations include roasted garlic aioli, herbed aioli, lemon dill aioli, and a list as long as your creative brain can imagine!

PREP TIME: 5 minutes **INACTIVE TIME:** 2 hours **YIELDS:** 2 cups

Herbed Aioli

INGREDIENTS
- ¾ cup mayonnaise
- ¾ cup parmesan cheese
- ¼ cup diced fresh chives
- 2 tablespoons chopped fresh basil
- 1 tablespoon chopped fresh rosemary
- 1 clove fresh garlic, chopped
- 1 teaspoon freshly cracked black pepper
- ½ teaspoon chopped fresh lemon thyme

DIRECTIONS
Mix and refrigerate for at least 2 hours before using. This aioli keeps for up to 3 days in your refrigerator. Put it on anything!

PREP TIME: 5 minutes **YIELDS:** 1 cup

Strawberry Basil Vinaigrette

INGREDIENTS

3 large, ripe strawberries
½ cup chopped fresh sweet basil
3 to 4 tablespoons champagne vinegar
½ teaspoon freshly ground black pepper
½ teaspoon salt
½ cup light olive oil

DIRECTIONS

Add all but the olive oil to a food processor. Pulse until smooth, and slowly stream in oil. Serve immediately on a fresh green salad with goat cheese and toasted nuts! It's delicious!

PREP TIME: 5 minutes **YIELDS:** 1½ cups

Signature Citrus Vinaigrette

INGREDIENTS

1 tablespoon honey

Juice and zest of 2 lemons

1 teaspoon salt

1 teaspoon freshly ground black pepper

1 tablespoon spicy brown mustard

Juice of 1 small sweet mandarin or tangerine

¾ cup good olive oil

DIRECTIONS

Whisk honey, zest, salt, pepper, and mustard into a paste. Slowly stream the juices into the mixture. Working quickly, stream olive oil into the dressing, and whisk continually to form an emulsion. The dressing will come together and begin to thicken slightly. Store tightly covered for up to 1 week in the refrigerator. Bring dressing to room temperature before serving.

PREP TIME: 5 minutes **YIELDS:** 1½ cups

Lime Cilantro Dressing

INGREDIENTS

4 limes
1 tablespoon honey
½ tablespoon Dijon mustard
Salt and pepper to taste
½ cup chopped cilantro leaves
1 cup good olive oil

DIRECTIONS

Juice and reserve 1 tablespoon of zest from the 4 limes. Combine honey, mustard, salt, and pepper in a bowl. Whisk in lime zest, then juice. In a slow, steady stream, drizzle in olive oil, continuing to whisk. Fold in chopped cilantro, and enjoy!

PREP TIME: 5 minutes **YIELDS:** 1½ cups

Meyer Lemon Caesar Dressing

INGREDIENTS

Juice of 1 large or 2 small Meyer lemons
3 to 4 anchovy fillets, packed in oil
2 egg yolks
1 teaspoon Dijon mustard
1 teaspoon freshly cracked black pepper
1 cup light-tasting oil
¾ cup finely grated parmesan cheese

DIRECTIONS

Blend all the ingredients except the oil and cheese in a food processor. Once that's creamy and blended, slowly stream in the oil until the dressing begins to thicken. Be careful to not overmix. Once the dressing is thick and creamy, fold in parmesan cheese. Eat this on everything, but especially on a Caesar salad!

PREP TIME: 5 minutes **YIELDS:** 1½ cups

Arugula Pesto

INGREDIENTS
3 cups young arugula
¼ cup cashews (or any nuts you have)
1 large clove garlic
¾ cup olive oil
3 tablespoons fresh lemon juice
½ cup grated Grana Padano cheese
Salt and pepper to taste

DIRECTIONS
Layer the ingredients in the order they appear in the recipe in a food processor. Pulse a few times to bring it together. Continue to pulse until you have a smooth pesto that looks a bit oilier than a traditional basil pesto.

This pesto should be especially runny in texture, as it's best for pairing with pasta or grilled meats or fish.

PREP TIME: 5 minutes **YIELDS:** 1 cup

Chive Oil

INGREDIENTS
1 cup extra virgin olive oil
½ teaspoon freshly ground black pepper
½ teaspoon salt
½ cup diced fresh chives (with blossoms, reserved, if tender and available)

DIRECTIONS
Add oil, salt, and pepper to a food processor. Sprinkle in chives. Pulse only a few times to create a beautiful green oil with many pieces of chives still recognizable.

This delicate oil can be used on top of meat, fish, and salads or even as dipping oil for bread. If available, use the reserved blossoms as a final garnish. The floral, soft onion blossom is a beautiful addition to any finished dish.

PREP TIME: 5 minutes **YIELDS:** 1 cup

Tangy BBQ Sauce

Homemade BBQ sauce was one of the very first things I ever learned to make. I can remember being around eleven years old, and my mom called out which ingredients went in the bowl next. She would give direction with, "A large squeeze of this and a sprinkle of that." The sauce was never the same, and that's what made it so special. She used to pour it over wings or chicken thighs and bake them till they fell apart. We'd eat it on a big bowl of steamed white rice. It was one of my favorites.

INGREDIENTS

¾ cup ketchup

¼ cup loosely packed dark brown sugar

¼ cup mustard, any style

2 tablespoons tamari or soy sauce

1 tablespoon apple cider vinegar (more if you like a tangy punch)

1 tablespoon olive oil

1 tablespoon tomato paste

2 cloves fresh garlic, crushed

1 teaspoon freshly cracked black pepper

DIRECTIONS

Simply combine all the ingredients, and you're done! If you want a milder garlic punch, cook it on the stove for about 10 minutes, and all the flavors will mellow and combine beautifully!

This sauce is great for a marinade or as a condiment. It'll last in your fridge about 5 to 7 days for your BBQ needs, or you can pour it on chicken to bake for a few hours, or spoon it over rice once your protein is finished cooking!

Closing Thoughts

Never be afraid to create. No matter how hard it might seem to start, follow your dreams, follow your heart, and never stop pushing, never stop believing that you were made to dream and accomplish great things. Failure is only a reminder that you're alive!

It's my hope that you will find something to love within these pages, that one of my recipes will become your own memorized specialty, that you'll add or take away an ingredient or two to create your own perfect meal. And I hope that your meal will be enjoyed for years to come by people you love. I want you to feel amazing each time you make it.

Truth be told, that's the beautiful thing about food: I believe that when heart, soul, and creativity are interjected into a recipe, no two people will ever make it the same. Every meal is uniquely yours.

Never stop cooking and creating, using your heart first. In a world where social media pressures us to prove to everyone that our lives are happy and magical, I will let you in on a secret: your life is happy and magical with all its flaws, and all its failed cheesecake attempts. It is brilliant.

The best parts of my life are no longer my achievements; they are seeing my son, Noah, light up every morning because the world is new for him, or hearing his twin cousins knock at the door to play. The boys swing the pantry door wide open, looking for a snack. Their tiny hands reach up to the table for fresh fruit, and we watch *Finding Nemo* in my living room for the millionth time.

This is what life is about: little people, with glowing, happy, excited eyes, eating the cake you thought was a failure and asking for just one more tiny piece.

The everyday journey is a gift, and every day, you've got an opportunity for joy. All the best in the world to you.

Special Thanks

Book Production

Michael Kartes
Dianna & Michael Hawkins
Jenny & Zachary Stennes
Jeff & Sonja Hobson
Christy Feltman
Ruthy & Andy Taylor
Sandy Deneau Dunham
Holly Holman
William Hawkins

Recipe Testing

Kelly & Matt Harber
Breanna Smithson
Crystle Ardoin
Dasha Bozhko
Stef Winter

Index

Note: Page numbers in *italic* refer to photographs.

A

aioli
    Herbed Aioli, 262
    Sun-Dried Tomato Aioli, 261

appetizers, 27–51
    Bacon-Wrapped Dates, *30*, *31*
    Black Bean Hummus, *32*, *33*
    Brie Bruschetta with Seasonal Fruit, *46*, *47*
    Cheese Boards, *28*, *29*
    Creamy Artichoke & Spinach Dip, *40*, *41*
    Pico de Gallo, *42*, *43*
    Rosemary & Bacon Flatbread, 48, *49*
    Spicy Baked Hominy, *44*, *45*
    Stuffed Roasted Apricots, *38*, *39*
    Sun-Dried Tomato Hummus, 34, *36–37*
    Tomato Basil Bruschetta, *50*, 51
    White Bean Puree, 35, *36–37*

apples
    Apple Cranberry Crisp with Vanilla Pouring Cream, 192
    Creamy Coconut Apple Strawberry Popsicles, *212*, 213
    Spiced Caramel Apple Pie, 234, *235*

apricots
- Perfect Apricot & Chocolate Chunk Oatmeal Cookies, 193
- Stuffed Roasted Apricots, 38, 39

Artichoke & Spinach Dip, Creamy, 36, 37
Arugula Pesto, 270

asparagus
- Asparagus & Cherry Tomato Panzanella, 54
- Roasted Yukon Golds with Asparagus & Rosemary, 86, 87

B

Bacon-Wrapped Dates, 30, 31
Balsamic & Tomato Jam, Quick, 255
Balsamic Dressing, 54
Balsamic Reduction, 31
Banana Bread Made with Greek Yogurt & Pepitas, 190, 191

bars
- Cream Cheese Pumpkin Pie Bars, 206, 207
- Tart Cherry Dark Chocolate Granola Bars, 242, 243

BBQ Sauce, Tangy, 271

beans. *See also* hummus
- Rosemary & Tomato White Beans, 84, 85
- Turkey & Chickpea Greek-Style Pitas with Dill Yogurt Sauce, 122, 123
- White Bean Puree, 35, 36–37
- White Bean, Sausage & Spinach Soup, 110, 111

beef
- Beef Barcelona Stew, 94, 95
- Beef Bourguignon, 97
- Classic Chili with Tomatillos & Grass-Fed Beef, 126, 127
- Perfect Braised Chuck Roast, 138, 139
- Stuffed Cabbage Rolls, 130
- Wine-Drenched Beef Short Ribs, 142, 143

beverages. *See* drinks
Biscuits, Black Pepper Buttermilk, 55
Blackberry Mint Water, 162, 163
Blood Orange, Fennel & Pistachio Salad, 56, 57
Blood Orange Whiskey Cocktail, 164, 165
Blueberry Muffins with Lemon Shortbread Crumbles & Buttermilk Glaze, Buttermilk, 228, 229
Blueberry Pie, 232, 233
Bread Pudding, 194, 195
Bread Pudding French Toast with Strawberry Syrup, 238, 239
Brown Sugar Cream, 197
Brownies, Almond Butter, 188, 189

bruschetta
- Brie Bruschetta with Seasonal Fruit, 46, 47
- Tomato Basil Bruschetta, 50, 51

Butter & White Wine Sauce, 129
Butter, Garlic Cheddar, 257
Buttercream, Infamous Chocolate Sandwich Cookie, 200, 201
Buttermilk Glaze, 229
Buttermilk Ranch Dressing, 260

C

cabbage
  Cilantro Cabbage Slaw, 70, 71
  Quick Sauerkraut, 256
  Stuffed Cabbage Rolls, 130
cakes
  Buttermilk Vanilla Pound Cake, *196*, 197
  Strawberry Lemonade Cake, *220*, 220–221
Carrots, Brown Butter, *58*, 59
Cheese Boards, *28*, 29
Cherry Dark Chocolate Granola Bars, Tart, *242*, 243
Cherry Ginger Beer Margarita (Ginger Beerita), *176*, 177
Chicago Dog, *157*, 159
chicken. *See* poultry
Chile Verde, Roasted Tomatillo, *106*, 107
Chili with Tomatillos & Grass-Fed Beef, Classic, *126*, 127
Chive Oil, 270
chocolate
  Almond Butter Brownies, *188*, 189
  Chilly Hot Chocolate, *166*, 167
  Chocolate White Chocolate Chip Cookies, *198*, 199
  Dark Chocolate Salted Almond Bark, *214*, 215
  Infamous Chocolate Sandwich Cookie Buttercream, *200*, 201
  Old Fashioned Drinking Chocolate, *178*, 179
  Perfect Apricot & Chocolate Chunk Oatmeal Cookies, 193
  Tart Cherry Dark Chocolate Granola Bars, *242*, 243
Cilantro Lime Dressing, *266*, 267

Cinnamon Rolls, New-School, 202, *203*
Cioppino, Pico de Gallo, *104*, 105
Citrus Tart, 210
Citrus Vinaigrette, Signature, *264*, 265
cookies
  Chocolate White Chocolate Chip Cookies, *198*, 199
  Coconut Custard Macaroons, *204*, 205
  Infamous Chocolate Sandwich Cookie Buttercream, *200*, 201
  Perfect Apricot & Chocolate Chunk Oatmeal Cookies, 193
  Pistachio Orange Shortbread Cookies, *226*, 227
  Sticky Marshmallow Toffee Cookies with Black Hawaiian Sea Salt, *244*, 245
Corn Bread, Garlic & Cheddar, 81
Couscous with Avocado & Slivered Almonds, Herbed, 68, *69*
Cream Cheese Pumpkin Pie Bars, 206, *207*
Crème Brûlée, Espresso Crusted, 216, *217*
Crème Fraîche Strawberry Bourbon Shake, *168*, 169
crisps & crumbles
  Apple Cranberry Crisp with Vanilla Pouring Cream, 192
  Lemon Shortbread Crumble Topping, 229
  Plum Crumble, *222*, 223
  Rhubarb & Raspberry Crisp, 237
Cuban Dog, *156*, 159

D

Danielle's story (introduction), 1–13
Dates, Bacon-Wrapped, *30*, 31
desserts. *See* sweets
Dill Yogurt Sauce, 120
dressings. *See also* vinaigrettes
    Balsamic Dressing, 54
    Balsamic Reduction, 31
    Buttermilk Ranch Dressing, 260
    Lime Cilantro Dressing, *266*, 267
    Meyer Lemon Caesar Dressing, *268*, 269
drinks, 160–181
    Blackberry Mint Water, *162*, 163
    Blood Orange Whiskey Cocktail, *164*, 165
    Cherry Ginger Beer Margarita (Ginger Beerita), *176*, 177
    Chilly Hot Chocolate, *166*, 167
    Creamy Bourbon Float, *170*, 171
    Crème Fraîche Strawberry Bourbon Shake, *168*, 169
    Espresso Ice Cream Float, *172*, 173
    Fresh Minted Limeade, *174*, 175
    Ginger Lemon Soda, 181
    Old Fashioned Drinking Chocolate, *178*, 179
    White Sangria, 180

E

eggs
    Deconstructed Prawn Niçoise Platter, *62*, 63
    Farro with Roasted Tomato Vinaigrette & Poached Eggs, *136*, 137
    Frisée Salad with Hazelnuts & Crispy Fried Egg, *66*, 67
    Poached Egg, 137
    6-Minute Egg, 64

F

Farro with Roasted Tomato Vinaigrette & Poached Eggs, *136*, 137
Fennel, Blood Orange & Pistachio Salad, *56*, 57
fish. *See* seafood
Flatbread, Rosemary & Bacon, 48, *49*
Frangipane Jam Tart, *208*, 209
Fruit Chèvre Tarts, Stone, *240*, 241
Fruit, Seasonal, with Brie Bruschetta, *46*, 47

G

Ginger Beerita (Cherry Ginger Beer Margarita), *176*, 177
Ginger Lemon Soda, 181
Graham Crackers, Homemade, 211

H

Ham & Brie Sandwich, 132, *133*
herbs, pantry, 17
Hominy, Spicy Baked, *44*, 45
Hot Chocolate, Chilly, *166*, 167
hot dogs
    Chicago Dog, *157*, 159

Cuban Dog, *156*, 159
Hot Seattle Dog or Drunk Dog, *157*, 159
Kraut Master, *157*, 159
Picnic Dog, *156*, 159
Southern Italian Dog, *157*, 159

Hot Seattle Dog or Drunk Dog, *157*, 159

hummus
Black Bean Hummus, 28, *29*
Sun-Dried Tomato Hummus, 34, *36–37*

I

Ice Cream Float, Creamy Bourbon, *170*, 171
Ice Cream Float, Espresso, *172*, 173
introduction (Danielle's story), 1–13

J

Jam, Quick Balsamic & Tomato, 255
Jicama & Lentils, 72, *73*

K

Kraut Master, *157*, 159

L

Lasagna, Creamy, Spicy Tomato, 152
Leek & Bacon Tart, Caramelized, *120*, 121
Lemon Curd, 220

Lemon Ginger Soda, 181
Lemon Simple Syrup, 249
Lentils & Jicama, 72, *73*
Lime Cilantro Dressing, *266*, 267
Lime Strawberry Pie, 236
Limeade, Fresh Minted, 174, *175*

M

Macaroons, Coconut Custard, *204*, 205

main dishes, 113–159
Angel Hair Pasta with Roasted Summer Veggies, *116*, 117
Baked Copper River Salmon with Spicy Pineapple Salsa, *146*, 147
Brown Sugar Ribs, *118*, 119
Caramelized Leek & Bacon Tart, *120*, 121
Cast-Iron Paprika Prawns, *124*, 125
Chicken Sausage & Tortellini Pasta Salad, 153
Classic Chili with Tomatillos & Grass-Fed Beef, *126*, 127
Creamy, Spicy Tomato Lasagna, 152
Farro with Roasted Tomato Vinaigrette & Poached Eggs, *136*, 137
Fettucine in Caper & Parmesan Cream Sauce, 128, *129*
Fresh Pasta with White Wine & Butter Sauce, 131
Ham & Brie Sandwich, 132, *133*
Hot Dogs, 156–157, *158*, 159
Lemon & Greek Basil Roasted Chicken, *134*, 135
Perfect Braised Chuck Roast, 138, *139*
Quick Cashew Chicken, *144*, 145
Spanish-Style Braised Chicken, *154*, 155

Spicy Kalamata Puttanesca, *140*, 141
Strozzapreti in Gorgonzola & Pancetta Cream Sauce, *150*, 151
Stuffed Cabbage Rolls, 130
Thai Rice Salad, 148, *149*
Turkey & Chickpea Greek-Style Pitas with Dill Yogurt Sauce, 122, *123*
Wine-Drenched Beef Short Ribs, *142*, 143

Mayo, Spicy Brown Mustard, 130
Minestrone, Sister's Turkey, *108*, 109
Mint Blackberry Water, *162*, 163
Minted Limeade, Fresh, 174, *175*
Muffins with Lemon Shortbread Crumbles & Buttermilk Glaze, Buttermilk Blueberry, *228*, 229
Mustard, Apple Cider Honey, 254
Mustard Mayo, Spicy Brown, 130

N

Niçoise Platter, Deconstructed Prawn, *62*, 63

O

Oil, Chive, 270
oils, pantry, 17
Onion Soup, French, 102, *103*

P

pantry staples, 15–23
Panzanella, Asparagus & Cherry Tomato, 54
pasta
    Angel Hair Pasta with Roasted Summer Veggies, *116*, 117
    Chicken Sausage & Tortellini Pasta Salad, 153
    Creamy, Spicy Tomato Lasagna, 152
    Fettucine in Caper & Parmesan Cream Sauce, 128, *129*
    Fresh Pasta with White Wine & Butter Sauce, 131
    Orzo with Dill & Tomatoes, 74
    Sister's Turkey Minestrone, *108*, 109
    Spicy Kalamata Puttanesca, *140*, 141
    Strozzapreti in Gorgonzola & Pancetta Cream Sauce, *150*, 151
Pavlova, Almond, 187
Peanut Butter Ice Box Pie, *224*, 225
pesto
    Arugula Pesto, 270
    Sun-Dried Tomato Pesto, *258*, 259
Picnic Dog, *156*, 159
Pico de Gallo, *42*, 43
Pico de Gallo Cioppino, *104*, 105
pies
    Blueberry Pie, *232*, 233
    Butter Pie Dough, 233
    Peanut Butter Ice Box Pie, *224*, 225
    Piecrust & Pies, Tips for, 230–231
    Spiced Caramel Apple Pie, 234, *235*
    Strawberry Lime Pie, 236
Pineapple Salsa, Spicy Sweet, 145
Pitas with Dill Yogurt Sauce, Turkey & Chickpea Greek-Style, 122, *123*

plums
   Plum Crumble, *222*, 223
   Plum Preserves, *252*, 253
Polenta, Creamy Parmesan Soft, *60*, 61
Popsicles, Creamy Coconut Apple Strawberry, *212*, 213
pork ribs. *See* ribs
potatoes
   Roasted Yukon Golds with Asparagus & Rosemary, *86*, 87
   Whole-Grain Mustard/Shallot Vinaigrette Potatoes, *82*, 83
poultry
   Chicken Sausage & Tortellini Pasta Salad, 153
   Chicken Sausage Sweet Potato Stew, 96
   Lemon & Greek Basil Roasted Chicken, *134*, 135
   Quick Cashew Chicken, *144*, 145
   Sister's Turkey Minestrone, *108*, 109
   Spanish-Style Braised Chicken, *154*, 155
   Stuffed Cabbage Rolls, 130
   Turkey & Chickpea Greek-Style Pitas with Dill Yogurt Sauce, 122, *123*
Preserves, Plum, *252*, 253

Q
Quinoa with Chèvre & Arugula, Red, *76*, 77

R
Rhubarb & Raspberry Crisp, 237
ribs
   Brown Sugar Ribs, *118*, 119
   Wine-Drenched Beef Short Ribs, *142*, 143
Rice Salad, Thai, 146, *147*
Ricotta Cheese, Herbed Fresh, 248

S
salads. *See also* dressings
   Asparagus & Cherry Tomato Panzanella, 54
   Blood Orange, Fennel & Pistachio Salad, *56*, 57
   Chicken Sausage & Tortellini Pasta Salad, 153
   Cilantro Cabbage Slaw, *70*, 71
   Deconstructed Prawn Niçoise Platter, *62*, 63
   Frisée Salad with Hazelnuts & Crispy Fried Egg, *66*, 67
   Heirloom Tomatoes with Goat Cheese, 61
   Orzo with Dill & Tomatoes, 74
   Red Quinoa with Chèvre & Arugula, *76*, 77
   Strawberry & Goat Cheese Salad, 89
   Thai Rice Salad, 148, *149*
   Watermelon Salad with Feta & Cilantro, *88*, 89
Salmon with Spicy Pineapple Salsa, Baked Copper River, *146*, 147
Salsa, Spicy Sweet Pineapple, 145
Sandwich, Ham & Brie, 132, *133*
Sangria, White, 180
sauces, spreads & toppings. *See also* dressings; hummus; vinaigrettes
   Apple Cider Honey Mustard, 254
   Arugula Pesto, 270

Balsamic Reduction, 31
Brown Sugar Cream, 197
Buttermilk Glaze, 229
Chive Oil, 270
Creamy Artichoke & Spinach Dip, *40*, *41*
Dill Yogurt Sauce, 120
Fresh Whipped Cream, 251
Garlic Cheddar Butter, 257
Herbed Aioli, 262
Herbed Fresh Ricotta Cheese, 248
Lemon Curd, 221
Lemon Shortbread Crumble Topping, 229
Lemon Simple Syrup, 249
Pico de Gallo, *42*, *43*
Plum Preserves, *252*, *253*
Quick Balsamic & Tomato Jam, 255
Quick Sauerkraut, 256
Salted Toffee Sauce, *250*, *251*
Spicy Brown Mustard Mayo, 130
Spicy Sweet Pineapple Salsa, 145
Strawberry Mash, 219
Strawberry Syrup, 187
Sun-Dried Tomato Aioli, 261
Sun-Dried Tomato Pesto, *258*, *259*
Tangy BBQ Sauce, 271
Vanilla Bean Pouring Cream, 249
Vanilla Pouring Cream, 192
White Bean Puree, 35, *36–37*
White Wine & Butter Sauce, 129

Sauerkraut, Quick, 256
Sausage & Tortellini Pasta Salad, Chicken, 153
Sausage Sweet Potato Stew, Chicken, 96
Sausage, White Bean & Spinach Soup, *110*, 111

Scones with Warm Honey & Fresh Strawberry Mash, Cream, *218*, 219
seafood
    Baked Copper River Salmon with Spicy Pineapple Salsa, *146*, 147
    Cast-Iron Paprika Prawns, *124*, *125*
    Deconstructed Prawn Niçoise Platter, *62*, *63*
    Pico de Gallo Cioppino, *104*, *105*
Shortbread Cookies, Pistachio Orange, *226*, 227
Shortbread Crumble Topping, Lemon, 229
shrimp. *See* seafood
side dishes
    Black Pepper Buttermilk Biscuits, 55
    Brown Butter Carrots, *58*, *59*
    Cilantro Cabbage Slaw, *70*, *71*
    Creamy Parmesan Soft Polenta, *60*, *61*
    Garlic & Cheddar Corn Bread, 81
    Herbed Couscous with Avocado & Slivered Almonds, *68*, *69*
    Lentils & Jicama, *72*, *73*
    Parchment Paper Vegetables, 75
    Roasted Delicata Squash with Garlic, *78–79*, 80
    Roasted Yukon Golds with Asparagus & Rosemary, *86*, *87*
    Rosemary & Tomato White Beans, 84, *85*
    Whole-Grain Mustard/Shallot Vinaigrette Potatoes, *82*, *83*
Slaw, Cilantro Cabbage, *70*, *71*
S'mores, 211
soups, 91–111
    Beef Barcelona Stew, *94*, *95*
    Beef Bourguignon, 97
    Butternut Squash Soup, *98*, *99*
    Chicken Sausage Sweet Potato Stew, 96

Classic Chili with Tomatillos &
	Grass-Fed Beef, *126*, 127
Creamy Tomato Soup, *100*, 101
French Onion Soup, 102, *103*
Pico de Gallo Cioppino, *104*, 105
Roasted Tomatillo Chile Verde, *106*, 107
Sister's Turkey Minestrone, *108*, 109
White Bean, Sausage & Spinach Soup, *110*, 111

Southern Italian Dog, *157*, 159

Spinach & Artichoke Dip, Creamy, *36*, 37

Spinach, White Bean & Sausage Soup, *108*, 109

Squash
Butternut Squash Soup, 98, 99
Roasted Delicata Squash with Garlic, 78–79, 80

strawberries
Creamy Coconut Apple Strawberry
	Popsicles, *212*, 213
Crème Fraîche Strawberry Bourbon
	Shake, *168*, 169
Strawberry & Goat Cheese Salad, 89
Strawberry Basil Vinaigrette, 263
Strawberry Lime Pie, 236
Strawberry Mash, 219
Strawberry Syrup, 187

sun-dried tomatoes
Sun-Dried Tomato Aioli, 261
Sun-Dried Tomato Hummus, 34, *36–37*
Sun-Dried Tomato Pesto, *258*, 259

Sweet Potato Stew, Chicken Sausage, 96

sweets, 183–245. *See also* cookies; crisps &
	crumbles; pies; syrups
Almond Butter Brownies, *188*, 189
Almond Pavlova, 187
Banana Bread Made with Greek
	Yogurt & Pepitas, *190*, 191
Bread Pudding, *194*, 195
Bread Pudding French Toast with
	Strawberry Syrup, *238*, 239
Brown Sugar Cream, 197
Butter Toffee, 186
Buttermilk Blueberry Muffins with
	Lemon Shortbread Crumbles &
	Buttermilk Glaze, *228*, 229
Buttermilk Glaze, 229
Buttermilk Vanilla Pound Cake, *196*, 197
Citrus Tart, 210
Cream Cheese Pumpkin Pie Bars, *206*, 207
Cream Scones with Warm Honey &
	Fresh Strawberry Mash, *218*, 219
Creamy Coconut Apple Strawberry
	Popsicles, *212*, 213
Dark Chocolate Salted Almond Bark, *214*, 215
Espresso Crusted Crème Brûlée, 216, *217*
Frangipane Jam Tart, *208*, 209
Fresh Whipped Cream, 251
Homemade Graham Crackers, 211
Infamous Chocolate Sandwich Cookie
	Buttercream, *200*, 201
Strawberry Lemonade Cake, *220*, 220–221
Lemon Curd, 220
Lemon Shortbread Crumble Topping, 229
New-School Cinnamon Rolls, 202, *203*
Plum Preserves, *252*, 253
Salted Toffee Sauce, *250*, 251
S'mores, 211
Stone Fruit Chèvre Tarts, *240*, 241
Strawberry Mash, 219

Tart Cherry Dark Chocolate
  Granola Bars, *242*, 243
Vanilla Bean Pouring Cream, 249
Vanilla Pouring Cream, 192

syrups
  Lemon Simple Syrup, 249
  Strawberry Syrup, 187

tarts
  Caramelized Leek & Bacon Tart, *120*, 121
  Citrus Tart, 210
  Frangipane Jam Tart, *208*, 209
  Stone Fruit Chèvre Tarts, *240*, 241
toffee
  Butter Toffee, 186
  Salted Toffee Sauce, *250*, 251
  Sticky Marshmallow Toffee Cookies with
    Black Hawaiian Sea Salt, *244*, 245
Tomatillo Chile Verde, Roasted, *106*, 107
tomatoes. *See also* sun-dried tomatoes
  Asparagus & Cherry Tomato Panzanella, 54
  Creamy Tomato Soup, *100*, 101
  Heirloom Tomatoes with Goat Cheese, 61
  Orzo with Dill & Tomatoes, 74
  Pico de Gallo, *42*, 43
  Quick Balsamic & Tomato Jam, 255
  Roasted Tomato Vinaigrette, 135
  Rosemary & Tomato White Beans, 84, *85*
  Tomato Basil Bruschetta, *50*, 51
toppings. *See* sauces, spreads & toppings
turkey. *See* poultry

Vanilla Bean Pouring Cream, 249
Vanilla Pouring Cream, 192
Vegetables, Parchment Paper, 75
Veggies, Roasted Summer, with Angel Hair
  Pasta, *116*, 117
vinaigrettes
  Roasted Tomato Vinaigrette, 135
  Signature Citrus Vinaigrette, *264*, 265
  Strawberry Basil Vinaigrette, 263
  Whole-Grain Mustard/Shallot
    Vinaigrette Potatoes, *82*, 83

Watermelon Salad with Feta & Cilantro, *88*, 89
Whipped Cream, Fresh, 251
White Wine & Butter Sauce, 129

Y

Yogurt Dill Sauce, 120

286 INDEX

About the Author

Danielle Kartes

Danielle Kartes is an author and recipe developer living near Seattle, Washington, with her photographer husband, Michael, and their two sweet boys, Noah and Milo. Together, the Karteses run their boutique food and lifestyle company, Rustic Joyful Food. Rustic Joyful Food promotes loving your life right where you are, no matter where you are, and creating beautiful, delicious, fuss-free food with whatever you have available to you. Danielle appears regularly on national television and speaks publicly at events around the country.